A

Williamsburg Hornbook

By Felicity Wise

With Illustrations by Penelope Pride

Answers to 185 questions most frequently asked
by visitors to this city.

For Fern 1973

THE PRUDENT PRESS
Williamsburg, in Virginia

Printed in U.S.A.
Prestige Press, Inc.
Hampton, Virginia 23361

ACKNOWLEDGMENTS

To a complete Virginia lady who has forgotten more than Felicity will ever know, the author expresses gratitude for encouragement and constructive criticism. To the experts of divers departments of Colonial Williamsburg Foundation who kindly answered technical questions; to craftsmen and others who interpret Virginia's colonial experience; to the staff of the Foundation's Research Library who patiently led Felicity (by the hand in some cases) to information sources; to friends who cheered Felicity on in her trivial but, hopefully successful, efforts; to the Foundation's Training Department for forcing mountains of information into a molehill of ignorance (the author) a dozen years; and last (but certainly not least) to Felicity's husband who nobly refrained from exercising the male prerogative to forbid Felicity to publish this little volume which he has not yet read (accounting for probable numerous errors he would have noted), the author offers her appreciation—and apology.

If you publish a book, a parish curate accuses you of heresy, a college sophomore denounces you, an illiterate condemns you, the public derides you, your publisher renounces you, and your wine dealer cuts off your credit. I always add to my prayers, "Deliver me, O Lord, from the itch of bookmaking."

Voltaire

PREFACE

In bygone days this little village virtually slept some two-thirds of the year. But for the sounds of craftsmen, tradesmen, lecturing professors at the College, sermonizing Anglican ministers and vociferous disagreements between fractious fellows having too long occupied tavern taprooms, life generally was at a pace incomprehensible to us, their descendants.

Albeit, twice annually, during "Publick Times" when the Government sat, Williamsburg became a thriving miniature metropolis. In the spring and fall the population doubled, even trebled and all ran hither and yon on missions of politics, business or pleasure.

'Twas then that wealthy planters, frontiersmen, Scot merchants and all manner of visitors thronged into the city to buy, to sell, to barter, to banter, bet on horse races or attend (if of the privileged class) elegant balls at the British Governor's Palace. For then, we were Englishmen.

Life was so different in the days of our forefathers—fashions, manners, morals (? ?), convenience, comfort, health and even the pursuit of happiness.

But today, one can step back into that age vicariously. One can tred old brick or shelled paths and traverse cobblestones now bordering hard-surfaced streets said to have been as deep as they were wide when it rained here 200 years ago. One can delight in an 18th-century garden. And, as one recaptures the sights and sounds of those times, he can likewise recapture the smells. Sniff freshly baked bread and ginger cookies, bayberry wax melting for candle dipping, printer's ink, apothecaries' herbs and medicines, and the cabinet maker's seasoning woods. The olfactory senses may well recall a stench (now threatened to extinction unless large portions of the population return to the farms)—that of nature's lingering suggestion of the presence of oxen, horses, fowls and sheep. 'Tis wise, however, to walk cautiously (glancing frequently to the ground) when reliving the past olfactorily.

There will be, withal, much the visitor will not learn or understand unless, perforce, he inquires into it.

This little Hornbook is, therefore, dedicated to the noble purpose of saving the visitor the trouble of asking—and frequent embarrassment resulting from factual answers when he does. It is additionally dedicated to all those who have so patiently and multitudinously answered the questions since the beginning of this historic restoration. It makes no claim as an intellectual work unless, perchance, the author has accidentally been enlightening. On occasion.

Farewell then,
Felicity

v

Index of Subjects
(Alphabetical Order)

****

AMOUR

****

It is indeed a happy circumstance that a subject, so universally fascinating since the emergence of man, conveniently begins with the first letter of the alphabet. For it is in this manner the author intends to proceed with the information of this hornbook. It favors the writer still further in that the question is most likely to command the readers' instant attention to the contents!

Q. Did the English Governors sleep with their wives?

A. 'Tis very curious that we moderns seem somehow to feel that because times have changed, human nature has kept abreast. Alas, man whom God wrought, changes little in a basic sense—retaining much the same dispositions to love and hate, despair and aspire, produce and reproduce as ever he did. It, therefore, becomes baffling that so many visitors in the Governor's Palace inquire as to the personal habits of those men when beyond the closed doors of their nupital chambers.

Please permit the author this time to substitute honesty for uncontestable evidence. For, having not the occult power to see into the past, not to mention past bed chambers, the writer must decline to venture an absolute in this instance.

It appears reasonable to assume, however, from the prodigious amount of space allotted to the subject of love and marriage and/or the lack of it in letters, journals and even the learned writings of the day, the Governors who loved their wives most likely slept with them as is often the custom today.

But, having no reference from any of those governors who lived in the Palace (other than a bachelor who will be referred to later—see how we hold your interest), the author must be content to refer the reader to a perusal of THE SECRET DIARY OF COLONEL WILLIAM BYRD for parallel reading on the subject. If the illustrious and colorful Colonel's amorous proclivities were, in any way typical of the age as we suspect they were, the above mentioned work is both enlightening and something less than dull, if not shocking. It is available locally at likely places.

AIR CONDITIONING

Q. Are the exhibition buildings air conditioned?

A. Er a yes and no. Felicity feels that to evade this issue would serve to convince the visitor that scrupulous attention to authenticity in Williamsburg is suspect. The truth is, the restoration policy is to strive strenuously to remove unauthentic or distracting semblances of the 20th century. The fact is, however, this is the 20th century. In a sense, then, there has been embraced a practical philosophy of what might be termed "deceptive appearances" in such cases where necessity demands the convenience, comfort and protection modern technology provides in the matter of preserving antiques and people. Felicity would beg to add here, for the benefit of the young reader, that the word "people" (particularly those curiously costumed ones seen here) and "antiques" are not synonomous—necessarily.

Since air conditioning as we know it today was not in general use in the 1920's when restoration of the Colonial Virginia Capital began, none of the original or reconstructed buildings had it at first. Systems of controlling ·humidity, temperature, cleanliness and circulation (which more elaborate designation better salves the authentic conscience) were perfected in following decades. There is uncontestable evidence that antique furniture, fabrics and houses enjoy extended life expectancy if sequestered in a controlled environment. Being subjected to less change in temperature and humidity and shielded to a degree from pollutants (Felicity apologizes for the necessity of resorting to this modern term), valuables of antiquity warp, crack and generally deteriorate at a much slower pace.

It is with this singular consolation that preservation has been placed paramount to authenticity in this respect. Temperature and humidity systems have been installed in most of the major exhibition buildings, whether original or while being reconstructed. There is, of course, further precedent for this delicate decision. All buildings have been heated from the beginning. That visitors and employees in these buildings are benevolently rewarded with great comfort afforded by the preservation policy is obviously a happy by-product of what might be termed "judicious compromise".

It might be noted here, so far as is known to the author, there has yet to be one complaint from a visitor regarding this departure from authenticity.

ARCHAEOLOGY

Q. Why do they dig?

A. Archaeology affords positive proof of human record buried in the soil upon which man grows and within which his last remains are deposited. Fortunately, his material remains often lie just beneath the surface. If the soil has not been disturbed, an expert archaeologist can determine building foundations, locations of streets, paths and gardens and all manner of sites upon which craftsmen once plied their trades. And, most fortunate of all, archaeology often tells its own fascinating personal story.

For instance, deep in an abandoned well which had been filled in with refuse and unwanted things (as was the custom of that day) was found a man's shoe in an almost perfect state of preservation. From the way it had been worn down by it's long dead wearer, the experts could state with a reasonable degree of certainty, that the man had a decided limp and probably was the victim of some orthopedic accident or malformation. Therefore, archaeology does more than merely confirm what has been put down by man's pen in an old ledger or map.

The filling of dried-up wells could be said to have been responsible for curbing some 18th-century pollution. On the other hand, some of our ancestors paid little heed to pollution (indeed, they were not familiar with the term) and even dumped or tossed garbage in the streets if so inclined to this unsanitary practice.

Often, an old inventory can be confirmed by archaeology as shards (bits and pieces) of ceramics, porcelains, stemware, hinges, pipes, nails, and other artifacts found in the ground correspond to that listed in the written record.

The fascinating science of archaeology will extend to the future even though photography, audio and other visual technical recordings of our times leave little to ponder, other than why we are why we are. And, even archaeology is of little use in this respect. It is hoped the soil strata of our century will yield more interesting examples of our advanced culture than bottle caps and political campaign buttons.

It is noted by mothers in this area that little boys often develop a peculiar disease which they term "amateur archaeologyitis". The first symptoms generally appear in a rash of holes dug in the back yard. As the disease progresses, a collection of broken bottles, ceramic shards, rusty nails and hinges and the like, clutter the child's room. Fortunately the disease is not fatal, usually petering out within a year or two. 'Tis the mother who seemingly suffers the greater.

****

ARCHITECTURE

****

Q. Why do the old buildings of Williamsburg differ so from those of the same period in New England?

A. The first permanent English settlement in America was accomplished at Jamestown, six miles from Williamsburg, in 1607; albeit historians often failed to mention this with any enthusiasm until well into the 19th century. (Dear reader, please forgive Felicity—she is but a southerner and must be beneficently tolerated on some occasions). Those who came to Virginia shores were, for the most part, "adventurers", representing (in the beginning) a joint stock company in England. Their hopes were to find precious stones, metals, lumber and naval stores for England's ships. The mother country needed these materials as well as an outlet for her manufactures, plus more room for the people to live in England. "Mother then hoped (indeed prayed) much of her over-population would remove itself hence to the new world, send raw materials to England and later purchase a finished product in something of a barter economy. 'Twas called "the mercantile system" wherein the colonies of an empire existed for the benefit of the mother country.

Although England was sadly disappointed in the outcome of most of the enterprise in the beginning, the type of Englishmen who came to Virginia then were predominately members of what we might call "the establishment" and DID further the cause of the empire in their own way. They clung to England's fashions in architecture, furnishings and dress. Williamsburg's earlier structures (when the town was being carved from a wilderness) date from the time of William and Mary and Queen Anne, reflecting the taste of the times "at home". Later construction (during the reigns of three Georges until the Revolution) followed the prevailing fashions of "home" but were adapted to the southern American climate and living conditions. This is termed "Georgian".

Early settlers of the New England colonies, on the other hand, had not left the old world for adventure or visions of wealth and empire—but rather to be left alone to worship and live in their preferred way, outside the established Anglican Church. For in England at that time, Church and State was one. The hearty New Englanders, being outside the Establishment, brought with them little more than a few personal belongings and visions of a different life. They improvised when building their homes, churches and other structures (using native woods and stone) and found it to their liking. Having simpler taste—and decided distaste for the styles, manners

- 4 -

and morals of the old country—New England developed somewhat more functionally than fashionably. In other words, the people there were less occupied with what might be termed "tradition" and were more studiously concerned with providing meat for the table and sustenance for the soul.

The remaining "period" architecture in that area, then, reflects the quaint and charming, if less sophisticated, preference and necessity of their circumstances of life in early America.

Note: We ardently hope that last sentence will please all and offend none.

★★★

AREA

★★★

Q. How much of Williamsburg has been restored?

A. Astonishing as it is to most visitors, town planning is not modern. Williamsburg was laid out in just such a manner. Late in 1699, the College of William and Mary (then the one structure now referred to as the Wren Building) was completed and stood, lonely but stately, surrounded by a virgin forest. Approximately a half mile distant, down the old horse path running eastward along the crest of the ridge of this narrow peninsula between the rivers York and James, nestled the little 1683 Bruton Parish Church. The present one dates from 1715. Williamsburg then, as a seat of government, came to the two arms of a trivium: Church, State and Education, settling down in happy matrimony as the town developed.

Duke of Gloucester Street, as the main street was named, ran due west to east an approximate mile where the Capitol building was completed in 1705. Members of both houses of the legislature had met at the college until it was finished. Nicholson and Francis Streets (undoubtedly named by the Governor himself, he being Francis Nicholson) ran parallel to the wide Duke of Gloucester. All three of these main thoroughfares were sliced at intervals where cross-streets cut through them. The result was a convenient and attractive little village. The restored area today is roughly that of the original town—nearly two hundred acres.

Portions which have not been restored or reconstructed but lie within the historic area border, are either privately owned or cannot be restored for technical reasons. For instance, the first block in front of the college became a modest business section for the sleepy little town after the Capital moved to Richmond during the Revolution. Buildings went up and down, were enlarged or diminished, and at times, demolished—a phenomenon of "progress" familiar to all. However, man's churning of the earth disturbes the stratigraphy of the soil and renders archaeology invalid. The importance of archaeological record has already been covered; and, therefore explains why the first block before the college (known today as Merchant's Square) has not been restored. It does, however, offer the visitor all manner of services and wares within the attractive façade of an 18th-century English village.

Along the concrete ribbon approaches to Williamsburg today are official markers designating locations of once popular taverns, trails and other historic sites. Along these roads in a bygone day, could be heard sounds of planters' elegant carriages, wagons of the lesser sort and, finally, the marching armies of the Revolution. Today, these highways are dotted with every conceivable interesting enterprise to delight the passers-by and stoppers-in.

****

BATHROOMS

****

Q. Where were they?

A. It appears this is a matter of gravest concern to the visitor. The answer is as simple as it is sometimes astonishing to one asking the question. As we know them today, there were no bathrooms in the homes of our forefathers and mothers. Some distance beyond the houses (for obvious reasons) were the "Necessary Houses", usually secreted behind or enclosed within pleasing plant screening. Those of the wealthy class often were quite elaborate, frequently supporting a cupola on the roof, and might accommodate up to three. The middlin' sort and lower classes made out with less elegance in spite of the lack of any difference whatever regarding the activity within.

In the homes of long ago, there were the "chamber pots", so called perhaps because they were located generally in the bedchamber where there was little concern to hide them. Here too, social status and elementary economics dictated the appearance and materials of which the chamber pots were made. In the Governor's Palace, two solid silver ones are quite open to public view. But, lesser materials ranging from pewter to saltglaze (which will be identified when these questions are reached alphabetically) were more often used.

In the homes of those disposed to modesty, some pots were cleverly concealed within stools, the lids of which often were embellished with needlepoint, and hinged. Some chamber pots were located under the seat (removeable, of course) of the curious "corner chairs" visitors find so intriguing.

The wing chair sometimes doubled as a commode chair, the advantage of which is not immediately apparent to moderns who, having centrally heated homes, are not well acquainted with cold drafts.

The matter of disposing of the unmentionable contents of these quaint

little past pots again depended upon one's position in life. If wealthy, one's servant performed the distasteful task. If overly modest or poor, one emptied one's own.

Seemingly, the chamber pot of those days usually denoted serious business. Felicity has read the works of famous experts who indicate these items were inscribed sometimes with pious or edifying statements. There is some information indicating the opposite was often true. For there have been found examples of early chamber pots bearing certain unrestrained admonitions to remind the occupant to limit the time he or she may be exercising what might be termed "squatter's rights". (Oh, dear. Felicity is blushing now!) She does also recall seeing one in some museum collection whose owner could be said to have disliked the current King, that monarch's picture being painted within.

The other activity prevalent in bathrooms of our enlightened age—bathing, was of less urgency to our ancestors. For that matter, too much of this activity was actually frowned upon by many as being possibly injurious to the health.

Visitors in 18th-century houses notice delicate stands holding a small basin (roughly the size of a large soup bowl). Underneath, on a shelf near the floor but part of the stand, sits a dainty "bottle" designed to hold approximately one quart of water. The stand usually is complete with an additional round container which opens mid-way to reveal a soap ball. We are told these conveniences were in daily use by our forefathers. But serious bathing—that is all over and seated in a wooden tub of water—was undertaken in frequency proportionate to the individual's personal fastidious nature and degree of belief or disbelief in the harmful effects cleanliness might have upon him.

As always, one's life station dictated details in the use of the tub. Servants of the topping folk of the day carried, from outside kitchens, buckets of hot water. The tubs were placed in the bedchamber—and always near the fireplace when frigid weather rendered the whole affair more disagreeable to begin with. The bath would then proceed much in the same manner as today with the exception that the contaminated contents of the tub would have need of emptying by hand just as it had been filled earlier with clean water.

Small buildings with drainage systems often are found near fine colonial homes. It is thought some of these curious edifices were of early Italian or Turkish origin and termed "bagnios" (pronounced "banyos"). These were bath houses; although the same term otherwise indicated in some parts of the world, a less innocent activity. In the bagnios, however, the more aesthetic might shower, weather permitting. The general difference in the act of showering then and now is that we can turn a spigot and obtain a spray of water of desirable temperature; whereas they had a servant douse the bather by the bucketsfull, the temperature of which was a matter of chance. It seems this would have required a minimum modesty on the part of both participants.

In any event, it may be safe to assume the all-over bath was an occasion rather than part of daily routine we moderns so concerned with social acceptance regard necessary. This pleasures us in the happy thought that WE might be somewhat nearer to Godliness than were our ancestors, at least in THIS respect.

★★★

BEDROOMS

★★★

Q. Who used which?

A. This question comes from a majority of visitors both in the palace and other homes open to the public. In the case of the palace (which has a third floor containing eight bedrooms probably used by children, their nurses and guests) there lived nine families—at different times, of course. The third floor is not open to the public due to the inability of using the narrow stairway.

Seven of the governors were British and two, Patrick Henry and Thomas Jefferson, were governors of the Commonwealth of Virginia. Only one record regarding the use of a bedroom exists. Governor Naborne Berkeley, Baron Lord Boutetourt (pronounced "Botitot"), a bachelor, was reported in 1770 by THE VIRGINIA GAZETTE, to have passed away in the southwest bedchamber of the Palace.

Note: The still published VIRGINIA GAZETTE is the oldest active weekly newspaper in this country. Established in 1736, it features a colonial format and excerpts of news, both foreign and domestic, on the first page. A copy of THE GAZETTE for the week he may be in the area provides an inexpensive souvenir for the visitor to take home as a reminder of what we hope has been a pleasant visit.

Other than the newspaper report of Lord Boutetourt's unhappy demise, who used what bedroom is merely surmising. For instance, we cannot be sure which room in the George Wythe (pronounced "with") House was used by General Washington during his brief stay in September of 1781 as he planned the siege of Yorktown. And we can only guess it was the most commodious and attractive bedchamber in the Peyton Randolph House the French Commander, General Rochambeau, occupied at the same time. The aging Lafayette is thought to have used that same chamber in 1824 when he returned to Williamsburg for a visit, at which time he was honored at the ceremony at Yorktown on October 19th, the 43rd anniversary of that conclusive battle for American independence.

Q. Where did indentured servants and slaves sleep?

A. Generally, their quarters were located in close proximity to their duties. For instance, a nurse in the households of the well-to-do would most likely occupy a cot in the room with younger children trusted to her care. Cooks, stable attendants, laundry and kitchen servants and others involved with the household routine might occupy quarters above, below or within the "dependency" buildings in which they carried out their chores. Farm workers usually were quartered in clustered or row houses some distance from the main house.

Q. Where did craftsmen's apprentices and other non-servant workers sleep?

A. If they had no quarters elsewhere, they often slept in the home (usually a loft or sometimes basement room) or in one of the "dependency" buildings on the employer's property.

****

BEDS

****

Q. Why are the beds so short?

A. As stated when discussing the previous delicate subject, antique beds also are a matter of enormous curiosity to 20th-century visitors. The fact that beds, especially those with canopies and hangings, appear to be extremely short leads many people to believe our ancestors were a population of midgets. The truth is that people were, on the average, somewhat shorter than we are today. The probable reason is better nutrition. Today's foods are enriched deliberately (with the manufacturers' greatest concern for consumer well being) and affect humans much the same way plants and vegetables are benefited when well fertilized.

But to answer the question regarding the size of beds. Actually, in most cases, they are not THAT short. There were then, it is admitted, no standardizations of size which a manufacturing economy dictates today. Beds, therefore, like shoes and clothing, were made to accommodate the

user. Childrens' beds obviously were smaller. Adult beds, in most cases, were but little shorter than our modern standard length of 76 inches. Many, however, were considerably wider than the 54-inch standard double bed today and is one contributing factor to the illusion of shortness. For instance, the bed most often in question—the heavily carved and inlaid Elizabethan oak one in the Governor's Palace—measures 74½ inches in length and 60 inches wide. Further, it stands in a room roughly the size of a small modern apartment, has heavy hangings, great height, massive posts and lacks the firmly squared edges and precise margins of today's mattresses. All combined, the illusion is a square of approximately five feet.

Now, the next question in the probable event you were about to ask it: "What about George Washington; they tell us he was six-feet-three?" This, too, has a logical (at least to our ancestors) answer. In those days, the night air was believed by many to be unhealthy. During sleeping hours, the so-called "bad humors" could creep in and mingle with the other air. These humors supposedly were heavier than the regular air and would in the course of the night, sink surreptitiously to the floor and suspend themselves there with ominous portent to the breathing sleeper. Consequently, no small number of the population believed that propping on pillows, further supported by bolsters, would elevate their heads and decrease the dangers from lurking humors below.

This could explain why even taller predecessors needed less lengthy beds if they did not lie stretched out full length in them. It should be noted that our ancestors would have been spared this undue concern if they had known (as we of the enlightened age) that most illnesses are caused by nerves, or viruses, those terms not being known to them. Were they not fortunate in this respect, though?

Q. Why did they use curtains around the beds?

A. It seems that ornate bed hangings were in use in Europe by the 15th-century. In any discussion of this type, it is logical to assume more than one reason dictated usage. For instance, there are fashions in decorating and privacy (which the privileged, noble or royal seldom had). Servants came and went, tending fires, bringing bath water or going about some other less agreeable chore already referred to. And, even a king might feel uncomfortable if performing some little dalliance within the bed's confines if his chamber was (as was customary) crowded with ministers, lords, favorites and those who aspired to become one or the other. It must be added that heavy hangings kept out cold winter drafts and lighter ones for summer permitted some circulation of air while inhibiting circulating night insects. They would, undoubtedly, screen out some of the above mentioned "bad humors" in addition.

Q. What did they use for mattresses?

A. Most mattresses were fabric covers filled with flock, which term includes wool refuse, shearings of cloth or hair. Wealthy folk usually added a feather bed for greater softness. The lower classes, possessing neither mattresses nor feather beds, more often slept on piles of straw or dried grasses or even crushed cornhusks. Sometimes these materials were stuffed into a tick.

Q. Did they have springs?

A. Ropes generally took the place of modern-type springs. These were laced in something of a basket-weave pattern through holes in the head, foot and side boards and provided a somewhat resilient base for the mattress. Let us not forget those unfortunates who often ended up on a board platform-like contraption, or worse still, the floor or ground itself. They did not choose these uncomfortable conditions with any regard to some knowledge that their backs might have benefited therefrom.

****

BEGINNING

****

Q. When did Colonial Williamsburg begin?

A. The reader is excused if he finds it less than logical that Felicity mentions this at some length under the later subject of HOUSES. It is not the author's intention to frustrate the reader; but Felicity, being female, is unintentionally frustrating. Admittedly.

****

BLINDS

****

Q. Did they really have Venetian Blinds back then?

A. Yes, and quite a long time before that. It seems that Marco Polo introduced contrivances made in the Orient called "sun shades" into Venice in the late 1200's. Venetian craftsmen, impressed with those Marco Polo installed in his own palace, copied the idea using native woods cut in convenient flat slats. This may have suggested the movable feature they perfected which permitted the blinds to remain in an up or down position with adjustment of light and air according to the slant of the slat.

By the 14th-century, Venetian Blinds were in use in fine homes in Europe. And one Joshua Kendall, House Carpenter and Joiner, advertised in THE VIRGINIA GAZETTE here in 1770 that he: "likewise makes the best and newest invented Venetian Sun Blinds for windows, that move to any position so as to give different lights, they screen from the scorching rays of the sun, draw up as curtains, prevent being overlooked, give a cool refreshing air in hot weather, and are the greatest preservative of furniture of anything of the kind ever invented."

Venetian Blinds were listed in Lord Boutetourt's inventory and in the records of Anthony Hay, an owner of the Raleigh Tavern. Mr. Jefferson removed them from the Palace in Williamsburg to be taken to Richmond when the Capital moved.

There has been little change in Venetian Blinds in all this time with the exception that most modern ones substitute metal slats for the usual basswood and Oxford cedar, much used in the 18th century. It is the author's opinion that there is some ignominious disgrace in our technical age when men can walk or ride on the moon while their wives are back on earth wiping Venetian blind slats individually (or taking them down altogether) to soak them in the bathtub for want of a better way to clean them.

****

BOWLS

****

Q. What are all the big bowls we see?

A. The subject of less commodious wash basins has been covered in a previous section. The very large bowls seen in the Palace, homes and taverns (usually in the center of a dining table) were punch bowls. If the reader has read the earlier information herein on the subject of bathing, a cursory comparison of the size of wash basins and punch bowls will tend to convince one of our ancestors' possible preference for liquids internal, as opposed to external.

Q. What about all those little bowls with a piece broken out of the rim?

A. These quaint containers were barber or shaving bowls. They were made of divers materials ranging from ceramics to metals and do, indeed, look as if someone had taken a large bite from their upper circumference. This semicircular indentation was, however, diliberately fashioned to permit the bowl to be held under the chin, allowing it to fit neatly around the neck during the shaving ritual.

We find some shaving bowls had small holes in the rim through which, presumably, a ribbon would be passed, permitting the shaver who possessed neither servant nor dexterity to tie the bowl around his neck, thereby leaving both hands free for the operation.

Q. What are the bowls with the open work or latticed covers?

A. These, we are informed, generally held hot steamed chestnuts, a gourmet delicacy of the past. Alas, chestnuts are so rare in our times, most moderns would not recognize one if they saw it.

Wash Basin   Punch Bowl
****

BOXES

****

Q. What are all these big boxes with a hinged top?

A. These boxes referred to are seen at the Capitol. It appears their ancient designation was "Bible Box". Earliest printing presses (dating from the 15th-century) were concerned primarily with religious matters; but all early printing was vastly expensive and books were regarded as precious possessions. (Note: Isn't it a happy thought that some people still regard them so?) These boxes generally were ornately carved, some fitted with pigeonholes to create a portable desk. Some had flat tops, others slanted ones, which created a comfortable writing surface if placed on a low table. Could they not, then, have been the origin of the piece of furniture we know as a desk?

There is further evidence that even in Puritan New England, some such boxes often shielded forbidden frivolities such as ear "wiers" and other such "wicked apparel". The large triangular ones, dear readers, most often held a gentleman's tricorn hat.

Q. What are the leather boxes with a handle on top?

A. Dispatch boxes, or for greater clarity, depositories for letters, messages and notices intended for delivery elsewhere—hence, the handle.

Q. What are the small metal boxes often seen on a mantle?

A. Usually flint boxes. We will mention matches later.

Q. What are the elaborate boxes we see in the bedchambers with brass or bead decorations?

A. Ladies, dear ladies, for shame! These were for jewelry.

★★

BRICKS

★★

Q. Where did they make bricks in the 18th-century?

A. Frequently, in colonial Virginia, bricks were made on the building site from the earth dug for cellars and foundations. They were formed in wooden molds and baked in kilns fired with hardwoods abundant here. There have been found what could be termed commercial sites which operated in those days to furnish bricks for builders (now known as contractors; but were then called "undertakers").

Note: See how Felicity manages to retain the reader's interest through this informative alphabetical encyclopedia of useful and useless information? You will find "Undertakers" listed elsewhere before the V's, W's, X's, Y's and Z's of this work if you care to pursue the subject.

There can be seen in this area a reconstructed brick-making site showing a "pug" mill where clay and other ingredients were mixed. This mill is operated by horse power, which term is here used in its generic sense and should not be confused with that power upon which we moderns rely to propel us across land, sea and sky at prodigious speed. Being a pug mill horse we venture to suggest, would be a boring labor. It would follow, perhaps, that two important qualities were desirable for this equestrian: to wit, strength and few outside interest. If any. It should be noted (for Felicity is an animal lover) that extraordinary attention is paid to the comfort, whims and working schedules of these horses, most of whom fare better than you and I.

Q. Where were the bricks made for Williamsburg's reconstructed buildings?

A. In the general area here and using the same ancient methods in order to produce the obvious authentic results.

Q. Why are some of the bricks shiny and almost black?

A. The soil hereabouts abounds in a certain mineral commonly called silica (Silicon diosice). The darker bricks simply resulted from baking or firing in the intense heat nearest the center of the kiln, uniformity of heat production not being part of their technology; and the glaze is just that— a melting of the silica which formed a glass-like surface. The use of these "deviates" apparently was the result of frugality and/or aesthetic sensibility on the part of former brick masons who, rather than discarding them, incorporated them within the building pattern which produced an undeniably interesting effect.

Q. Why are the lighter bricks laid in fan-like patterns around and/or above windows and doors?

A. Brick houses had very thick walls (of solid brick) which lent them to the treatment of interior shutters (see shutters later). To relieve an austere façade and embellish brick structures with an artistic touch, brushed or gauged bricks (cleaned by scraping and brushing) were used to outline windows and doors. This was another fashion borrowed from the mother country.

Q. Why are brick steps usually bordered with wood?

A. Old brick, as has been explained, could not be fired uniformly at tremendous heat intensity and were softer, more porous and more easily broken than our modern ones. A hardwood border prevented chipping and, thus, delayed the step-replacing problem.

****

BURGESS

****

Q. Where did the term "Burgess" originate?

A. Historically, a burgess was an inhabitant or freeman of an English borough (county). The term was applied to a respresentative of a borough, corporate town or university in the British Parliament. The word comes from the old middle English "Burgeis" (equivalent to burg) and was, in the two colonies of Virginia and Maryland, a representative to the popular or elected branch of the legislature. In Virginia, as in England, there were burgesses from certain towns and one from the College as well as two elected to represent each county.

Note: It is hoped this scholastic definition will not, to any appreciable degree, disillusion or disappoint hundreds of modern visitors bearing the family name Burgess and are visibly delighted at the Capitol Building to consider themselves descendants of such an ancient and august body.

Q. How many burgesses were there?

A. This depended on the particular year in question. As stated, there were two from each county. As new counties were formed due to the increase in population and settlement, the membership of the House of Burgesses increased accordingly. In 1699, when the Capital moved from Jamestown, there were 52. According to English custom, the College was permitted one burgess as was the town of Williamsburg by 1722. In 1736, Norfolk was awarded the privilege.

At the time of the Revolution, the body had grown to the enormity of 130. Since that time, some 18th-century counties are now in other states, Virginia having ceded western and northwestern territory which now forms seven other states. Today, Virginia has 96 counties, some having been incorporated with others and otherwise redesignated. And the lower house of the modern legislature is termed the House of Delegates or Representatives.

****

CANDLES

****

Q. How did they light them?

A. Guides in Williamsburg are obliged to answer this question with such frequency, the amiably include answers to two more which invariably follow the first: "How do you put them out?" and "How did they change them?"

Long metal poles (shaped much like a shepherd's crook) hold a long, waxed taper and are equipped with a snuffer. The taper is, and was lit and the candle-lighter went then and now goes about his overhead task much in the manner of ceremonial church lightings. The snuffing is accomplished in precisely the same way, using the cone-shaped accessory to smother the flame. Changing candles in lanterns or chandeliers too high to be reached by standing on the floor is as elementary as it is simple. One merely stands on a ladder, which useful contrivances have been in existence in some form or other since man's early beginnings.

Q. What were the candles made of?

A. The lesser folk found it necessary to use animal fats and oils referred to as tallow. Candles were a major household expense and bother. Bayberries supplied an excellent and pleasingly scented wax with an additional advantage in that it is an attractive natural earth-green color. Beeswax candles also were much in use. And, there is considerable evidence that fine pure white spermaceti candles, made from the waxy solid obtained from the oil in the head of a sperm whale, were ordered from England by affluent Virginia planters. Spermaceti candles are NOT in use in Williamsburg today, however, due to the threatened biological extinction of the great sperm whale. And it is with the same diligence so assiduously attended to in preserving the past, that Williamsburg is no less concerned in matters of modern conservation.

★★★

CAPITAL

★★★

Q. Why did it move from Jamestown?

A. By 1699, the tiny village on the James was ninety-two years old and no less innoxious to the inhabitants' health than the first settlers found it to be. Selected unwarily, they had not realized their chosen site was, in fact, a low, swampy peninsula and bountifully productive of every specie of worrisome insect and fever.

Further, on the eve of the 18th century, the population was ever venturing inland, taking up new lands and forming new counties. Moving a mere half dozen miles in those early days brought the government closer to the center of the governed. The last straw, or rather the last fire, was to be the immediate determining factor for the move at the time.

The fourth State House at Jamestown had been consumed in flames, the same fate of the first three; and a new one had to be built anyway. The odious hazard of fire explains why the new Capitol in Williamsburg was constructed without fireplaces. The Government and the Court met in

April and October when the weather in Tidewater is generally mild and salubrious. Heat, then, could be if not always happily at least bearably, relinquished. In addition to the foregoing reasons for the first move, the high ground of this narrow peninsula was esteemed as a "healthful location". It was well drained and, as has been mentioned earlier, was the location of the College and Bruton Parish Church.

Q. Why did the Capital move from Williamsburg to Richmond?

A. For one of the same reasons it was moved the first time—to go further inland, closer to the still westward moving body politic. It would be vastly deceptive, however, should we not mention the most expedient reason at the moment—that being the presence of British war ships in both the York and James Rivers. Their guns were aimed menacingly toward the town. For this was in 1780 when America was suffering birth pangs and the war had come to Virginia.

During the Virginia campaign in 1781, culminating with the decisive American victory at Yorktown in October, the Government found it necessary to seek temporary capitals (sometimes rather quickly) and sat at Charlottesville and Staunton before returning permanently to Richmond.

Q. What did they use this Capitol Building in Williamsburg for after the move to Richmond?

A. After the battle of Yorktown, the old building echoed the moans of wounded men as did most of the public buildings which were used as military hospitals. Later, it was used briefly as a boys' school and still later, as an office building. Provisions for heating had been added and eventually, in 1832, the building succumbed to flames.

Devoted members of the Association For The Preservation Of Virginia Antiquities acquired the property and preserved the foundations of the old building as an historic shrine until the restoration of the town, through private funds, made it possible to reconstruct it. Thus, bricks which once supported the first elected legislative assembly in America (the Virginia House of Burgesses) yet serve as the foundations for the authentic replica building.

* *

CARTER'S GROVE

* *

Q. How far is it to?

A. Approximately six miles east of Williamsburg.

Q. Is it worth driving down there to see?

A. But, of course, it is! Carter's Grove is one of the finest original Georgian period mansions in America. It was built in the mid-18th century by the grandson of the wealthy and prolific, Robert (King) Carter. Privately owned many, many years, it is now open to the public.

The Seatlantic Corporation (a Rockefeller enterprise dedicated to saving threatened historic houses) purchased it and later presented it to Colonial Williamsburg Foundation. It is hoped the visitor will eventually see it as a complete operating 18th-century plantation with cultivation of crops and crafts preserving a bygone way of life.

****

CERAMICS

****

As with furniture and trees, specialized books are available many places here to give technical and complete information on this broad subject. However, not to include a few questions so often asked by the visitors, would be nothing less than gross neglect by your conscientious, if non-intellectual author.

Q. What is Delft?

A. Delft, so called because it was being made from the first part of the 17th-century in Delft, Holland, is a base of common clay fired with a tin enamel glaze. It was one of many European attempts to imitate the appearance of the much desired but imported Chinese porcelains. Most people think of Delft as being blue. It was, however, made in brownish, mulberry and even polychrome decoration. Nor was it made only in Holland.

The English copied it and called it Delft; and some Dublin (Ireland) pieces are on display in Williamsburg. In France, the same ceramic was termed Faïence. The process was known in the ancient near East. Majolica, as it is termed in Spain and Italy, is merely another name for the same ceramic.

Q. What is slipware?

A. Another early ceramic made of a good red or brown clay and fired at a very low temperature. It would be "slipped" then into a thin, colored mixture of clay and refired. Designs were added by decorating with additional clay on this later coat of "slip", or by scratching through it and allowing the darker clay underneath to show through. This is termed "Graffito".

The predominately yellow and brown ware seen in Williamsburg is slipware. It is still made here by an independent potter as are saltglaze pieces. This delights the collector unable to afford the antique counterparts.

Q. What is Saltglaze?

A. 'Tis just that, dear reader—a common ceramic, the glaze of which is formed when salt is thrown into the kiln as the pieces are being fired. Gases are created from the salt and the sand which has been added to the clay before firing, all of which forms the glaze. Most saltglaze seen in Williamsburg is recognizable by it's greyish-blue color (often with darker blue decoration); but more sophisticated white saltglaze pieces are not uncommon and are recognized by the minutely pitted effect on their surfaces. This is created when the salt is thrown into the kiln.

Q. What are all these animal figurines?

A. Most of them are termed "Whieldon" or "Whieldon type" because it was an English potter, Thomas Whieldon, who became known for the mottled and tortoise-shell decorated pieces. If a guide answers "Whieldon type", he or she means "copied from Whieldon" as opposed to "made by"; for many potters copied his work.

Whieldon did make the lovely pieces on the mantle of the small dining room of the Governor's Palace. These are agate ware, formed by mixing different colored clays together which permits the decorative effect to go through the entire body of the piece rather than being painted on.

Q. So much is said about Chinese porcelain. Didn't they make porcelain in England?

A. The Chinese had practiced this art since the 9th century. The English did not learn how to achieve the desirable translucent ware until the middle of the 18th century; and then, their pieces were what is termed "soft paste" as opposed to "hard paste", and were inferior to the Chinese pieces. When English craftsmen learned much later what the Chinese had known for centuries, they began to create fine porcelain as the Orientals had been doing— by using Kaolin with Feldspar rather than with ground glass. The Chelsea and Bow factories produced the earliest English "hard paste" porcelain; but it was not until the early 1800's that English porcelains came into their own.

Note: Queensware and Creamware (both rather sophisticated ceramics) were made in England of a purer, whiter clay with the use of transfer printing as a means of decorating. Much of these wares were shipped into the United States after the Revolution in an English attempt to recapture the American market.

****

CEILINGS

****

Q. Why were they so high?

A. Once an eager youth answered this question before the guide could reply to the guest who asked it. He spontaneously offered the obvious (to him) but incorrect information that the ceilings were high because the furniture was. Of course, the truth is the contrary. Massive furnishings were designed proportionate to spacious rooms and high ceilings. In England, massive rooms and high ceilings went hand in hand with elegance and grandeur. And England's Virginia mimics, as was earlier mentioned, delighted to live in a style to which their grander and more elegant relatives "at home" were accustomed.

A second and singularly practical reason for high ceilings was the heat of southern summers which are hotter hot than the winters are colder cold.

Note: Felicity begs the kind reader's indulgence. There is no deliberate attempt at obscurity here. In fact, 'tis a fascinating phenomenon that females so frequently exalt the imagination in "a manner of speaking". Thus, if some reader of the stronger (if less expressive sex) finds the foregoing perplexing, Felicity suggests he ask the nearest female to explain it. If she fails to understand it, we are presumptuous enough to conclude THAT individual of the fairer sex does not think like a female in the first place.

In this unhappy event, Felicity hastens to explain: Southern summers are relatively hotter than the winters are cold. The problem of winter heat loss in high-ceilinged rooms, then, was less irksome when contrasted to the greater comfort afforded by increased circulation and the rising of hotter air to the high ceilings in summer. Those who could afford such construction were more than happy to permit as much heat as chose to rise and hover above their heads rather than to enfold them, as in a damp warm blanket, at the level of their activities.

```
********************************************************************
```

CHILDREN

```
********************************************************************
```

Q. Where do all these groups of children come from?

A. From far and wide actually. The majority, of course, are Virginia students and the tours here are part of their study program in the Commonwealth's history. Specially trained "Escorts" are provided for this educational experience. Many other groups come from nearby states and the District of Columbia; but numerous others (especially High School and Scout groups) travel many hundreds of miles to visit Virginia's past.

    Note: We respectfully remind the regular visitor who may feel enveloped (yea, even besieged) by the numerous groups on some days, that the children we may save (as respecters of their heritage) may be your own childrens' children. Isn't that a lovely thought?

```
********************************************************************
```

CLEANING

```
********************************************************************
```

Q. How did they dry clean fabrics in the 18th century?

A. The actual process of dry cleaning was discovered in France about mid-19th century and has been perfected considerably since that time. In the days before commercial dry cleaning, the fullers and dyers advertised their ability to "clean and scour" fabrics. Wet cleaning began with brushing and was followed by the traditional soap and water method. To remove stains and clean fine fabrics which could not be subjected to wet cleaning, a number of mentionable (and one somewhat unmentionable) substances were used and are here listed: butter, milk, turpentine, lemon juice, soda, gin (it would be devilish good fun to don a garment recently cleaned by this method), alum, new laid eggs (oh dear—but then, 'twould be better than old ones), white vinegar AND ox gall! One might be repelled when dancing with a gentleman, handsome though he may be, whose clothes were so odiously cleaned.

Q. How do they clean the old fabrics in the collection today?

A. Ver . . . ry care . . . ful . . . ly! Felicity jest. But 'tis true. The old fabrics are gingerly placed in a modern conveyance and delivered to a firm in a distant city whose business it is to clean museum fabrics. The author does not know their secrets.

****

CLOSETS

****

Q. Where did they hang their clothes?

A. Closets as we use them today were rare in the 18th century. Where they existed, they usually held bulk storage or had pegs for hanging heavy capes, hats, great coats and night clothes. Most other clothing was folded carefully and laid in drawers, which explains another frequent question: "Why did they have so many chests of drawers?"

This train of thought, like the ones on beds and bathrooms, proliferates a variety of related questions. For example: "Who did all the ironing?" This question is NEVER asked by a man. But, again, the answer is simple. If wealthy, one's servant did it. If of the middlin' sort, one did it one's female self. If very, very poor and not concerned in the least with social ostracization, some slept in what they wore (which might be their total wardrobe) and cared not a whit for wrinkles and other subsequent unpleasant conditions.

Q. How did they get those big wide dresses in drawers?

A. When the reader progresses to the subject of costumes, this will emerge as no problem. For the dresses were not wide. It was that which was worn under the dresses that was wide. And we hasten to mention the term "Farthingale" lest some modern ladies who are calorie conscious gleefully consider themselves manifestly more attractive in contrast to their supposed wide-hipped foremothers.

Note on closets: In her youth, Felicity once read a forbidden novel which hinted that closets, in those less than prudish times, were used in European Courts and noblemens' manors (on occasion) by certain gentlemen who should not have been where they were before they hastened to the nearest closet for reason of expedient exist. However, Felicity knows this was never the case in colonial Virginia.

****

COAL

****

Q. Did they really have coal?

A. Wood was so plentiful and so easily obtained, most people used it; but the wealthy class often bought coal. Coal was found in many parts of the colony. Colonel William Byrd II (who was interested in a multitude of things in addition to amour under which subject he was mentioned earlier) was investigating a possible coal mining operation at Falling Creek as early as 1709. The first American (coal) mine was opened near Richmond in 1745 and records show that coal from Virginia was shipped to Philadelphia to help make arms for General Washington's army.

Many of the upper class used coal by mid-18th century. It was what was referred to as "pit coal" (as distinguished from charcoal) or "sea coal" as a name for mineral coal. Coal was imported from Great Britain (sent as ballast in ships) and was advertised for sale in the VIRGINIA GAZETTE at various towns and landings.

****

COMMONWEALTH

****

Q. What is a?

A. The official designation, rather than "state" (they, however, being the same thing) of Virginia, Pennsylvania, Massachusetts and Kentucky (which last was part of Virginia until after the Revolution). It is merely another way of denoting "the body politic in a state in which supreme power is held by the people". The term is precisely the same in meaning to "common-weal" or the common welfare, or public good.

Perhaps, it having a more "democratic ring" at the time of the Revolution, one need muse but briefly upon the political proclivities of these now Commonwealths at that time and it would appear, they might have adopted the term then in order to be more emphatically emphatic!

****

COSTUMES

****

Following bathrooms and beds, costumes are of most enormous interest to Williamsburg guests. We could not hope to list and answer all questions on the subject nor in any order particularly significant to the public's prodigious interest. The following seem to be asked most frequently.

Q. Who makes them?

A. Colonial Williamsburg has a Costume Department employing numerous ladies, all expert seamstresses and tailoresses. (Note: Felicity takes pride; she knows of no other author having used the word "tailoresses"). A "block" is prepared for costumed guides in exhibition buildings, the block being a pattern cut to an individual's measurements. The costumes are made by hand with only essential stress areas sewed on modern machines.

Q. How many do you have?

A. This depends on the employee's schedule. Those ladies who work a regular forty-hour week usually have seven.

Q. Who cleans them?

A. Colonial Williamsburg has a laundry and dry cleaning staff; therefore, this disagreeable task (if it were the responsibility of the wearer) is taken care of as is all maintenance and repair.

Q. Are they comfortable?

A. Yes, and No. (We promised to be honest). One makes a somewhat difficult adjustment at first; but this is soon accomplished. Certain restrictions in "cut" do not always lend themselves to the 20th-century figure as much as the wearer might wish. Most of the questions, however, seem to be connected with the weather. Therefore, in answering the "comfort" question in this respect, Felicity honestly admits that when wearing costume in an air-conditioned building on hot summer days, the answer is "yes". Conversely, if walking to exhibition buildings on cold winter days when the wind is blowing, the answer is "no".

Q. Are they authentic?

A. Yes, indeed, which is another reason the answer to the foregoing question is occasionally "no". 'Tis a subject too delicate for Felicity to enlarge upon. However, old prints and portraits of the period are studied with great care and prodigious research in museums containing many examples of existing 18th-century colonial fashions was undertaken. Fabrics, of course, are modern but always reproductions of some typical design of that period.
    Note: Felicity divulges a secret. Gentlemen (particularly those past forty) frequently comment on their preference for the colonial fashions for females as compared with some of today's most popular styles.

Farthingale

Q. What are those things on your hips?

A. This question, naturally, is always addressed to the ladies. Those "things", as earlier mentioned are termed "Farthingales", and were worn off and on (there is no pun intended) from the 16th century. The name comes from an ancient term for tree-shoot, or rod. Therefore, they were so called because of the term "rod"—to extend the skirt. The contraption bears resemblance to two bucket halves turned upside down and covered with fabric. These are fastened to a band which fits about the waist.

Those early ones generally were constructed of reed or wooden bands; but their modern reproductions are less fragile, being fashioned with narrow steel strips, bent to shape. This is yet another judicious compromise in an age when ladies are busied with many tasks and spend little time in sequestered parlors with their needlework. In fact, ladies wearing farthingales in Williamsburg today are most likely busy conducting you, dear reader, through historic buildings.

The larger farthingales were hinged to allow milady to fold them up under her arms, permitting her to pass through doorways head-on. As the style waned, or for less formal wear, farthingales were smaller and did not require hinges. It is to be assumed, however, that ladies who might have been as wide without farthingales as those more delicately proportioned were with them, would have been obliged to enter doorways sideways when wearing either style.

Q. What are the little ruffled caps called?

A. These frivolous female embellishments were known as "Butterfly Caps" because they would, quite literally, fly away if not pinned on. The style was a remnant of a less frivolous day and an ancient religious notion that women should keep their heads covered. In the 18th century, they were merely fashionable and retained not one reminder of piety. They were worn by females of the upper class and even under large bonnets without which no lady would have ventured forth into the sun.

Mob caps, on the other hand, were commodious gathered circles of cloth covering the entire head. Since they were worn (before the Revolution) most often by the ordinary housewife or servant, 'twould be safe to assume they had something to do with protecting the tresses from dust and odors of wood smoke for those who performed the, then necessary and now fashionable, activity of fireplace cooking.

It would be added that when the Revolution broke out, English styles became symbols of Toryism and both Butterfly caps and farthingales gave way to fashions following a more democratic direction.

Q. Why did the men wear wigs?

A. Felicity does not wish to offend; but it is a simple fact that males have ever been subject to vanity as are females; and mens' wigs were merely fashionable as they had been long before the 17th and 18th century in ancient Egypt. They became popular in Europe in the 17th century, were at the height of fashion during the reign of France's Louis XV, and the style was waning somewhat by the 1790's. It was not until after 1800, when long hair for men went out of style, that wigs became popular for ladies of the upper class. Thus, colonial men who wore wigs were simply keeping up with the English Joneses who were keeping up with the French Louises.

Note: Felicity exercises admirable restraint in not including here a lengthy dissertation regarding history repeating itself.

Q. Why did they powder the wigs and with what?

A. Fashion again, gentlemen. The white wigs were for formal wear and were powdered with a mixture of starch and plaster of Paris pulverized to a fine white dust. The author has been unable to locate reference to what might have happened to gentlemen so surmounted if caught in a sudden downpour without a hat.

White wigs are still worn in English courts today, a lingering traditional and nostalgic official dress of the legal profession there.

Q. What did the ladies wear under all that skirt?

A. Felicity blushes. But, the bare fact, according to a learned modern expert (indeed several) in the matter of 17th century and 18th century dress is—oh, dear, this IS embarrassing—but we might say—well, it appears we MUST say—scarcely anything! There now, that's over!

We must, in all fairness, add that the educated in this subject of under-dress maintain the practice of under-underdressing was true of both sexes. Indeed, if one studies the old engravings of "tell it like it was" artists (Hogarth, for instance) or reads old diaries of the period, one cannot but be convinced of the validity of the above answer.

However hesitatingly, the author hastens to inform the agast readers that people seen in 18th-century dress in Williamsburg are not required to conform to authenticity beyond range of your vision. She also notes with some curiosity herself, that visitors never ask about gentlemens' underwear—unless, of course, they only ask gentlemen.

Q. What are the little capes worn by the ladies?

A. These are "tippets" and served much the same purpose as the modern sweater. Longer, hooded overcapes are referred to as "great capes" and the term "cardinal" is used to distinguish the ankle-length hooded capes, possibly because they resemble the brilliant red ones traditionally worn by ecclesiastics of that degree.

****

CRAFTS AND CRAFTSMEN

****

After diligent research, it was discovered the question most often asked of the craftsmen here is, "What are you doing?" This, craftsmen say, is a very happy indication the visitor is interested in their labors and further affords the artisans an excuse for lengthy discourse on the subject closest to their hearts—their arts.

Williamsburg now has approximately thirty crafts, many of which are quickly dying in our technical age. Thusly, it can be said, there is being created here "a climate for craftsmen", who while performing their crafts, earn their living doing what they most enjoy. Additionally, they are preserving the fact that there is a dignity and pride connected with making a thing of beauty or utility with one's hands.

A few specific questions noted by some of the craftsmen are listed here.

Q. At the basket weavers' shop: What kind of wood do you use?

A. White oak; and a basket expertly woven of split white oak can be handed down for generations in usable condition.

Q. To the candle dipper: How many times do you have to dip the taper in the hot wax to produce a candle?

A. If making bayberry candles, between 25 and 40 times; for beeswax, approximately 20 will suffice.

Q. The shoemaker and harness maker are most often asked: What kind of thread are you using to sew through that leather?

A. Generally flax; although, in the 18th century, hemp was sometimes used.

Q. At the blacksmith: Why aren't you shoeing horses?

A. Williamsburg's noted 18th-century blacksmith was Elkanah Deane, a fine coachmaker and producer of all manner of necessary decorative and useful items for home and farm. He had apprentices and journeymen and one of these was in the business of shoeing horses. This matter of equestrian footwear was but a minor part of Mr. Deane's business which, the visitor will note, was rather prosperous. He lived in the substantial two-storied white frame house fronting on Palace Green and his formal gardens were equal to many more ostentatious dwellings.

Felicity smiled, as will the reader, to have been told by the present counterpart of Elkanah Deane, that visitors really ALWAYS wish to know where his chestnut tree is. Alas, he does not have one; but there are other fine shade trees casting cool shadows over the red hot coals and leaping flames within the shop.

Q. What is a cooper?

A. A cooper makes barrels, then a moŝt necessary item for all farm, household and business use. And the cooper's craft is almost a bygone art. Fortunately, there are master coopers in Williamsburg (captured from England) whose own forefathers had been coopers for decades.

We add, lest a visitor be unduly shocked upon hearing of a "wet" cooper or a "dry" cooper. These are terms used to distinguish the craftsman who made barrels tight enough so as to retain liquids (thus, a wet cooper) or barrels for grain and other dry materials (a dry cooper). The terms "wet" and "dry" do not apply physically as a characteristic of the craftsman himself unless, of course, one views them in ratio to the weather and strenuous labor the craft requires. In this case, a hard working cooper on a hot day would, most likely, be a somewhat wet cooper regardless of which type barrels he might be making. Conversely, a wet cooper would, quite literally, become very dry if forced too long to abstain from liquid refreshment of the type for which his barrels were made. Incidentally, should the reader's last name be Cooper, the foregoing discussion does not apply in any event. Necessarily.

****

DANCING

****

Q. What kind of dances would they have danced here in the ballroom?

A. Colonial Virginians were not a prudish people, albeit they were much concerned with niceties and manners. A glamorous evening at the Governor's Palace may have begun with a stately minuet. But, as the evening advanced and as good friends, music, food and drink blended, one can be reasonably certain that lively reels and quadrilles (even jigs, after a few trips to the punch bowl) would have enlivened the affair.

It seems that entire families often attended parties and balls. Obviously everyone did not dance at once. The "Supper Room" for refreshments would have been a popular place; and lantern-lit gardens (weather permitting) provided a pleasant setting for moonlight strolls.

Felicity recalls reading in some 18th-century traveler's journal that the "ladies of Virginia are inordinately fond of dancing; but I must admit they are rather good at it." And, one English Governor, in an official report, declared "there is not an ill dancer in my society." The tall young Burgess (and later President George Washington), not famous for being at ease with the fairer sex, has been said to have danced once for a period of three hours without stopping.

Dancing

****

DEBTORS

****

Q. If debtors were put in prison, how could they pay their debts?

A. This is an enormously intelligent question. Felicity has wondered about it too. Mr. Jefferson considered it impractical; and he and others were sucessful later in bringing about legislation abolishing incarceration for indebtedness.

It should be pointed out that "gentlemen" in Debtors' Prisons were treated less perfunctorily than criminals who stole chickens or beat their wives. Traitors, murderers and arsonists, along with other more hardened of the criminal society, generally were quickly disposed of if convicted. But debtors, a great percentage of whom were of the wealthy (if insolvent) class, were permitted to receive food, blankets and other necessities from their distressed relatives and friends. This, of course, did not solve the problem of their indebtedness; but it DID permit them to worry in greater comfort.

- 33 -

DIARIES AND JOURNALS

★★★

Q. Why did so many people keep diaries and journals?

A. It is tempting to suggest it was a philanthropic gesture on the part of our ancestors to save us the trouble and expense of great research when reproducing their times. It is more probable, however, they took greater interest in the vicissitudes of daily life, noting particularly their more splendid moments, or (having no psychiatrists) pouring forth frustrations and heartbreak as a matter of pen and paper catharsis.

Today, we glean glimpses of the past which, otherwise, could scarcely be known. We learn of the human psyche of the period, as it were. They are the mind recordings of their day and abound in every matter of useful information just as their ledgers tell us what they bought, sold, paid for or charged.

A perusal of some of these personal records reveals at least two other interesting observations. Ladies, young and old, generally spelled abominably; and gentlemen, young and old, seemed generally more concerned with ladies, as such, than their spelling aptitudes. Felicity admits she, too, spells abominably; but this has in no way rendered her more appealing to the stronger sex. Regretfully.

★★★

DRINKING

★★★

Q. What were their favorite drinks?

A. Well, dear reader, we must be honest. It was NOT water; and this is discussed elsewhere. Water supplies, then unpurified as they are in our times, were suspect sources of dread diseases; AND colonial Virginians had a proclivity for alcohol. What they drank depended on taste and pocketbook. The wealthy could import fine wines from England, France, Spain and Portugal. Scotch and gin were imported and rum was a prevalent drink of the middlin' sort. Locally made beer, ale, wine and cider provided the alcoholic amenities for those who could afford nothing better.

We venture to comment that the practice of mixing some of the above mentioned beverages provided the most potent pleasures in an alcoholic state. There is an old recipe for Fish House Punch every connoisseur of strong constitution and intestinal fortitude should try if he has not already done so. Note a warning, however: the novice should abstain entirely. And other colonial favorites such as posset (hot milk curdled with ale or wine, sweetened and spiced) and caudle (warm wine or ale mixed with eggs, sugar and spices) should be avoided assiduously by all moderns.

Although our forefathers held great store in the medicinal benefits of posset and caudle when forced down the ailing, Felicity knows from sad experience these 18th-century "cures" more often cause 20th-century ailments which work just to the reverse. That is to say, these curious mixtures admittedly must be forced down; but there is no known force which will force them to STAY down. They are, to the contrary, most likely to reappear with the utmost dispatch.

Note: Bourbon was a late-comer in America, having been perfected by Virginia's stepchildren in Kentucky and, later, Tennessee (they being a more rugged and plainer sort who preferred strong drink straight and uncontaminated with such mundane ingredients as milk, eggs and spices).

****

DUKE OF GLOUCESTER

****

Q. Who was he?

A. He was one of Queen Anne's seventeen children, all of whom died in childhood. He lived longer than any of the others, dying in the year 1700 at the age of eleven. Since his mother was on the throne when Williamsburg was still in the building stage, it seemed altogether appropriate to honor her little boy by naming the main street of the new Capital for him. She died in 1714. Her husband, George of Denmark, is seldom mentioned, apparently having distinguished himself only by fathering seventeen children and living six years less than the woman who bore them.

****

DYES

****

Q. What were they made of and why do the colors last longer than ours?

A. Alas, man has always considered himself capable of improving upon that which God gave us. Dyeing fabrics is an ancient craft of centuries ago. The materials were those furnished by Nature herself rather than synthetics of our technical age. Literally thousands of barks, leaves, roots, nuts—even bugs, dear ladies, provided substances from which dye baths were made.

Use of a mordant (metallic compound combined with the organic dye bath) renders colors exceedingly permanent. Even more curious, if different mordants are used with the same bath, divers colors result. A revival of this ancient art could provide an altogether fascinating home hobby. For a modest start, gather goldenrod or save onion peelings (if one's family consumes several thousand hamburgers each year). Boil these separately, of course, to make a dye bath. Divide the baths and add different mordants, alum and iron sulphate for a start; then simmer ordinary untreated white wool yarn in each bath until the desired intensity of color is obtained. Later, if one be a knitter, fashion a multicolored scarf with the results. Doesn't that sound like fun?

****

ELECTRICITY
****

Q. Is there any in the exhibition buildings?

A. Oh, my, yes. But isn't it clever how the experts have concealed it from your view? One will realize it is absolutely necessary to provide this modern marvel (albeit it is getting so expensive) in order to install alarm systems as well as to furnish power for modern cleaning equipment (used only when the buildings are closed). And, in some cases, it renders dark stairwells safe for you, valued visitor. This is why you see the small half-dollar-sized holes in the ceilings you ask about so often. 'Tis but another necessary "judicious compromise".

****

EMPLOYMENT
****

Q. How do you get to work here?

A. We would find it abundantly pleasing if we could say each employee is sought out and enticed to add his or her particular skill, talent or ability

to the total efforts and purposes of the restored city. In many cases of unusual or unique talents and skills, this IS the case. It is more often, however
reluctantly we say it, that the employees have simply applied and were
placed or not placed (by Personnel Department) depending upon skills,
talents, abilities—or the lack of any.

Q. How many people work here?

A. Colonial Williamsburg has a year 'round employment force of approximately 3000. Seasonal increases, many of which are summer jobs for college
students and teachers, assist the permanent force when, alas, thou art all
here at once.

****

FABRICS

****

Q. Why do the old ones last so long?

A. The same answer applies here as was discussed in the subject of dyes.
For, natural fibers woven by hand in the tradition of true craftsmanship,
provide a superior product. Many of the old fabrics in the collection are
said to be in as good condition today as reproductions of them made some
thirty years ago when the second Colonial Capital was but an infant. Many
modern plastics, metalics and synthetics admittedly prove abundantly
satisfactory (and time and money saving) but are still less valued by individuals devoted to the preservation of natural materials and craftsmanship.
    Albeit, Felicity has no quarrel with table cloths requiring only a wipe
of a wet sponge or husbands' shirts needing not one touch of the iron. She,
therefore, trusts the modern fabric industry will recognize the impartial
exactitude with which she answered the oft' asked above question.

Q. Did they actually use these red and white and blue and white checks on
furniture?

A. This question is asked approximately three thousand times daily during
the months of June, July and August when shocked ladies enter the elegant
Palace ballroom, furnished with priceless antiques, some of which are
covered with woven checked fabrics. Felicity apologizes to those who would
wish to view the ballroom as it would have looked during the social season
(the spring and fall when the Government sat) when everyone of consequence would have been entertained here. But, alas, there is record that

summer dust covers were used to protect the elegant velvets, damasks and needleworks from the ravages of heat, humidity and, of course, dust.

One British Governor's inventory listed several dozen sets of these checked linen dust covers in the above colors. 'Twas an inexpensive fabric, usually bought by the bolt and used in servants' quarters, taverns and homes of the middlin' sort; but would have been on hand and available for the frugal and functional purpose of protection for finer fabrics. The visitor seeing the Palace in its summer garb will please accept the unfortunate fact that this record was found. 'Tis one more proof, however, of the attention to the most minute details of authenticity.

****

FINISHED

****

Q. Is the restoration of Williamsburg finished?

A. Nay, dear reader. You may return again and again to be greeted by yet another "new" old building, craft or activity. To mention but a few of the possible future projects, there may be reconstructed the home of Martha Washington's first husband (John Parke Custis), the Tyler house AND the first institution for the insane in America.

There have been overheard whispered conversations regarding the last mentioned possible reconstruction. It would appear the Hosts and Hostesses are somewhat uneasy regarding whether they shall be obliged to interpret this interesting building from without or within.

****

FIRES

****

Q. Did Williamsburg burn down?

A. Heavens, no! Please, kind reader, forbear—it is just that it pains Felicity to know how many people think some great conflagration once consumed the former Colonial Capital of Virginia in a matter of hours.

The truth is, Williamsburg is unique. For, there is no area in America today, so important a political center during the colonial period so abundantly intact. Standing still are some 88 original buildings. Other important colonial political centers such as Philadelphia, Boston, New York,

- 38 -

Charleston, Annapolis etc., developed into large metropolitan areas. Progress moved in and old buildings were destroyed, burned or crowded in among the new and are, therefore, now dispersed.

When the Capital moved to Richmond in 1780 during the Revolution, the little town slowly went to sleep, being then distinguished only by lingering memories of former glory and the prestigious College of William and Mary. Time passed, and seemingly passed Williamsburg by. Proud residents (many of them descendants of original inhabitants) were obliged if not content, to bask peacefully within the warm sheltering blanket of memories.

Fires occurred over the years, as anywhere, the result of what might be termed "natural causes" (sometimes better designated "human carelessness") with two notable exceptions. After the Battle of Yorktown, the Governor's Palace was used as a military hospital and was, in December 1781, consumed in flames and completely destroyed except for the old cellars which were full of tons of rubble from the original building when excavated in the late 1920's.

The magnificent old 1699 main building at the College (now known as the Wren Building) suffered a similar fire at that time as did the President's house. However, the damage to both was confined to their interiors and the old walls are intact. Other fires plagued these buildings, ravaging interior parts; but they stand today, used to the same noble purpose for which they were constructed over two hundred years ago. The Wren Building is shown to the public by Colonial Williamsburg guides with the generous consent of the College. The entire third floor and other rooms on the first and second still function academically as they have over 270 years.

****

FIREPLACES

****

Q. Didn't they have anything but fireplaces for heat?

A. Some form of stoves were made of clay, tile or earthenware since early Roman times. The earliest iron stove on record was found in a late 15th-century German castle. Dutch, Swedish and German settlers of the American colonies (especially in Delaware, Pennsylvania and New Jersey) brought iron plate stoves or molds for casting them. The Franklin stove was invented in 1743 and was in common use for a period after the Revolution. It is said stoves (until the approximate middle of the 19th century) generally were used as auxiliary cooking equipment and were almost always vented into the fireplace itself.

It appears our English ancestors in Virginia did not take to the strange devices with the notable exception that the Virginia House of Burgesses, in the year 1770, received "an iron stove" as a gift from British Governor Boutetourt. This curiosity, unattractive as it is, can be seen in the museum here. However, the visitor may fail to agree with its maker who modestly declared: "It excells in grandeur anything ever seen of the kind, and is a masterpiece not to be equalled in all Europe . . .".

Q. Why are there so many corner fireplaces?

A. 'Twas an ingenius method of cutting building costs. Moderns who build homes having fireplaces will quickly perceive that several openings, all drawing through one common chimney, would be a most frugal factor in this respect.

Q. What are those things in the fireplaces that look like coal chutes?

A. Another proof of our artisan ancestors' amazing ability. They are flues which, in corner fireplaces, were constructed at angles and funneled into the central chimney which served them.

Q. Didn't they have fire screens? (See Pole Screens)

A. Seemingly not. Fenders of iron, brass and steel provided some protection from popping coals and stray sparks. It should be noted that the lack of protective screens is one logical cause of frequent fires—which invariably leads to the next question.

Q. Why were the hearths usually so narrow then?

A. Please be generous, kind reader. Felicity has wondered about this too.

Q. What are the large flat iron squares back of the grates?

A. They are "firebacks" and served the very functional purpose of absorbing much heat which, otherwise, would have caused the soft and porous bricks of the times to crumble much sooner than they did.

It may be of particular interest to some that we have been told by some architects that the colonials relined their fireplaces frequently if they reached a dangerous condition. The fireplace openings, then quite logically, became smaller and smaller each time this repair was made over the years. If this condition is found before restoring an 18th-century building, it is corrected in the restoration process and the fireplace opening returned to it's original size.

Note: The most curious fireplace in a Williamsburg exhibition building is the result of a late 18th-century faux pas. Guests seldom ask about it, seemingly afraid the answer would be so simple as to embarrass them for their ignorance. It is located in a front upstairs bedroom of the fine old original Wetherburn's Tavern.

A later owner, after Mr. Wetherburn's death, noted the chimney needed to be replaced. He, therefore, hired a Mr. Humphrey Harwood to do the job. Now, Mr. Harwood's masonary ability is somewhat suspect; for as the architects proceeded with the restoration of this building, they discovered the chimney was leaning at the second floor level at such an angle the fireplace opening was no longer in juncture with it. Mr. Harwood's unconventional yet relatively uncomplicated solution was to create a new opening to the oblique. He then constructed a flu diagonally to reach and open into the tilting chimney, plastering over the entire affair, creating something resembling what would now be termed "Danish Modern".

It is not necessary to dwell upon the possible verbal reaction of the building owner, who, after all, bore responsibility for engaging Mr. Harwood's services in the first place.

****

FIREWORKS

****

Q. Did they have fireworks in the 18th century?

A. The Chinese developed fireworks as early as the 9th century and pyrotechnical displays have since been an important element of festivals throughout the world. Today, as in Williamsburg's glorious yesteryears, elaborate displays of these colorful and ingenious illuminations are a delight to visitors on special occasions including Christmas, New Year and other important events.

Authentic account of such notable celebrations date here as early as 1702, recorded in the words of a Swiss traveler who was witness to one such occasion at the College. That the "show" was not without mishap and even potential disaster is evident: "As part of the preliminary preparations, inquiry was made whether anyone knew how to set off fireworks. Several from the war ships volunteered . . . three grandstands were erected before the College where the fireworks were to be set off . . . the fire-master who was considered the most expert and boasted of his skill, was at the appropriate spot . . . but the results showed that he did not succeed in gaining much honor. In order to preserve his reputation, he acted as if the fire had fallen unintentionally into the fireworks, for he blew up everything at once in a big blaze of smoke. As there were all kinds of fireworks, many in large rockets, he like others, had to run and he had his clothes burnt."

Fortunately, no such harrowing experience has ever marred the visitors' obvious enjoyment of modern counterpart displays of this ancient diversion.

****

FLAGS

****

Q. Why does the British flag fly over the Capitol?

A. Williamsburg is for its guests, a visit to the past. The flag flying over the Capitol 315 days a year is the official British flag during the reign of Queen Anne, noting the union of England and Scotland. This obsolete flag is used because the Capitol was constructed during her reign.

On May 15, 1775, the Virginia Delegates in convention, adopted resolves to declare independence. Upon the unanimous "yea" vote, the British flag was pulled down from the building cupola and replaced with what the Americans termed the "Continental" flag (also the flag of the Great Union or the Cambridge flag) which bore thirteen alternating red and white stripes to denote the colonies. Even though this flag still featured the Great Union field in the upper left corner, it was the only one available at the time representing thirteen colonies.

Each year, from May 15th until July 4th when all thirteen colonies declared for independence, this Great Union flag flies over the Capitol and along the Duke of Gloucester street. This period is termed "Prelude to Independence". On the 4th of July, the current American flag is displayed proudly throughout the town. But on July 5th, again for the sake of authenticity in the visitors' colonial experience, the British flag of Queen Anne resumes its usual place. And the inhabitants once again return to their unique role of British subjects.

Note: The author hastens to assure the reader that playing this role for your enjoyment and edification in no way detracts from or disturbes their good traditional American loyalty and patriotism; for, indeed, its very roots form a firm mat just under the visitors' feet.

FLOORS

Q. What kind of wood are they?

A. The abundant southern long-leaf (Loblolly) yellow pine, or Pinus Taeda for the purist, which was cut from Virginia forests. Using wood cut edge grain in random widths, Virginia homes in the colonial days had flooring generally longer lasting than hardwoods of today. Proof of this is to note their condition after millions of people have walked over them since the first exhibition buildings were opened to the public in the early 1930's. Old flooring, salvaged from buildings beyond restoration, has been used even in reconstructed one. Please note: Although the guests are not permitted to sit on antique chairs, they are constantly walking on antique boards.

Q. Did they wax them in the 18th century?

A. Sometimes, probably with beeswax; but, more often, they were cleaned by industrious scrubbing and (if elegance were a matter of concern) covered with precious Oriental or English carpets.

Q. Do they wax them now?

A. Yes, with a heavy-duty commercial wax; but only to protect them from the daily punishment of thousands of tramping feet.

Q. Why do you use nails in the flooring?

A. Because they did in the 18th century. Remember, the tobacco economy dictated a barter system and English products were sent to Virginia in payment for her "golden weed". Thus, hand wrought nails were used, especially in the Tidewater region. Structures of the lesser folk on the frontier were quite a different matter. However, the ever resourceful Mr. Jefferson, when building his magnificent Monticello on the fringe of the frontier, had artisans making nails right on the property. This, of course, would have been vastly more interesting to Mr. Jefferson than merely transporting them from the coast.

FLOWERS

Q. Who arranges the flowers in the exhibition buildings?

A. Several talented ladies, trained in the art of 18th-century-style floral decorations, are at work each day long before most visitors have opened their eyes. These ladies prepare the exquisite embellishments to complement the beauty of their surroundings.

Q. Do the flowers come from the exhibition gardens?

A. Many of them do. There are additional cutting gardens outside the restored area to supplement the daily changes made when flowers are in bloom. During winter months, dried flowers are used as was the typical English custom of the day. And, these arrangements are prepared by the same ladies in advance of the winter winds. The dried arrangements add color; but many native Virginia evergreen foliage arrangements lend freshness to dreary winter months.

Q. Are the fruits and vegetables used in table arrangements real?

A. Indeed, they are, just as the fruits and greens used to fashion the fantastic window and door decorations during the Christmas season.

****

FOOD

****

Q. If wealthy Virginians ate meals of several courses lasting two hours at times, what did they eat all that time?

A. As today, what they liked best. Felicity suggests the visitors treat themselves to some of the colonial delicacies (including spoon and Sally Lund bread, peanut soup, hickory-smoked ham, fresh ocean Spot and others) still served in numerous local establishments. In this manner, one may visit the past tastefully. There are approximately 30 dining places in and near Williamsburg in what is here termed "Virginia's Historic Triangle"— Jamestown, where our nation began; Williamsburg, where the seeds of revolution were sown; and Yorktown, where the flower of the new nation bloomed in the defeat of the British October 19, 1781, in the decisive battle of the American Revolution.

Felicity does recall one criticism offered by a foreign visitor once traveling extensively in the colony. "I have traversed the length and breadth of this vast colony some three months now", he wrote, "and these Virginians have fed me both bacon and chicken at each and every meal until I fear if

I continue in this manner much longer, I will surely sprout bristles and feathers."

****

FREEHOLDER

****

Q. What was one?

A. In colonial Virginia, the term applied to a property owner who thus having "a stake in society", was possessed of all the rights and privileges of voting and holding public office under the Royal Charter of 1618. Please see "Burgess" also.

****

FURNISHINGS

****

Q. Are they reproductions?

A. Only rarely. The vast majority of furniture, fabrics, accessories, wall coverings, rugs and other equipment is antique. The term "original to the period", frequently used by guides, simply means "antiques" as opposed to "reproductions". This distinguishes, for the benefit of the visitor, that antiques are original but not necessarily original to the building he may be viewing at the time. This is only logical; for homes and public buildings, if not still occupied by the descendants of original owners, would seldom retain furnishings placed in them when they were first constructed. The Department of Collections, has one of the largest and most valuable acquisitions of antiques (English and American) in the country.

The few exceptions where some reproductions are used include the Capitol where various furnishings listed in old inventories are simply not to be found. For instance, the Capitol inventory listed 36 matching, carved, cane-backed chairs. Prodigious research has yet to locate such a number as those described and, thus, reproductions from the description of the originals have been used.

Another logical and obvious reason for exception is found where continuous daily use of antique tools would destroy them in a matter of days. Then, too, during periods of heaviest visitation when thousands of people tour the buildings daily, it is necessary to use reproduction fabrics in certain areas where the visitor may accidentally brush against or thoughtlessly touch ancient and priceless ones.

Felicity respectfully notes that it is an American custom to go about the business of shopping, testing a product's potential worth to the buyer by touching it. Alas, this is disastrous when commendable interest or curiosity leads thousands of viewers, who are NOT shopping, to forget and do what comes naturally.

We hope this point is kindly taken and will exonerate the guides. The frequent expression, "Please do not touch", is understandably a "touchy" subject, considering how many times the guests hear it. However, its very legitimate reason having been explained, we are confident, will eliminate the necessity for using it in the future.

Q. Is that a Queen Anne (Chippendale, etc. etc.) chair?

A. Pray, gentle reader, allow Felicity to digress as she is prone to do anyway. Antique furniture seen in Williamsburg ranges roughly from the Elizabethan and Jacobean period (early 1600's) through the styles popular in England during the reign of Charles I, the Cromwellian Commonwealth, and the reigns of Charles II, James II, William and Mary, Anne and three Georges.

In those less frantic times, styles took longer to reach popularity and distribution in the colonies and, once considered "stylish", remained so longer. Today, we retain furnishings of an earlier period than our own admitted generation (whether from economic necessity or sentimentality) and our forefathers did likewise. Thus, that which is slang in our day and often termed "Duke's Mixture" or "Early Married", had its counterpart even in the homes of governors and wealthy planters.

Those inquiring about chairs, highboys, lowboys, chests on chest, chests on frame and the like can find such excellent detailed information in books treating the subject as to render the author's limited knowledge and the number of pages allotted this little work ludicrous. If the reader is still with Felicity, note we are but in the "F's" even now.

Q. What do they use to polish and preserve the antique furniture?

A. Felicity snooped. She asked questions. Would you believe she begged? It appears the antiques are "fed" with a secret formula which retards the ravages of aging and renders antique beauty everlasting. 'Tis pleasing that good furniture can thus be saved the indignity of the aging process which humans must endure with philosophical fortitude.

It was ascertained, however, that such "feeding" compounds are commercially available. Further, it was learned that do-it-yourselfers wishing to preserve a natural wood grain finish on furniture not professionally finished, will find such inexpensive natural oils as olive oil excellent. Much rubbing and a good waxing at intervals helps.

Q. How did they finish the walnut paneling?

A. Official sources indicate numerous treatments have been used in recon-structed buildings such as the Capitol and the Palace. These range from oils, acid stains (acetic acid, the essential constituent of vinegar) with pig-ment, and prepared commercial stains. The Palace paneling has been rubbed with a lead mixing oil containing mineral spirits.

★★

Gaol

- 47 -

GAOL

Q. Where is the "gol"?

A. "Gaol" is the old English spelling for the same word we term "jail" and is pronounced precisely the same way. It is, however, located just down the hill to the left of the entrance door of the Capitol (if you are facing that door, otherwise to the right—that IS clear, isn't it?) And, yes, you will find the stocks and pillory there. Please do not leave your children.

Note: A very wise lady once told the author she had read, she knew not where nor when (for she has read so much) that the word "Gaol" originated as an English contraction of two words, "gay hole". This seems altogether probable since some ancient philosophical wag could have referred to it in this manner much as we use the term "hoosegow". Indeed, the authoritative Oxford English Dictionary mentions, in connection with the word "jail", an old English expression of a "deop (deep) gay hole". Now isn't that fascinating?

GLASS

Q. Why are the window panes so wavy?

A. They are blown glass, not a lost art. The Chance Brothers Company in Birmingham, England is still in business (well over two hundred years) and supplies Colonial Williamsburg with this authentic product. The huge blown glass bubbles are spun out at great speed so the centrifugal force flattens them somewhat. Pane-sized pieces are cut from the flattened portion and that which is left is remelted and the entire procedure repeated. Isn't it encouraging that this ancient and frugal practice of reprocessing glass is being revived by the more responsible members of the industry today?

The glass is wavy in the exhibition buildings because it bears evidence of the spinning process and is always somewhat concave or convex depending on which side one is looking through.

Incidentally, glass is nothing even so new as the 18th century. The earliest specimens were found in Egypt and date some 2000 years B.C.

Q. Is that Waterford?

A. Visitors frequently ask why they do not see fine Waterford chandeliers instead of the English or Irish "cut glass" ones here. Waterford, according to the Department of Collections, became famous for it's lovely pieces. They were made in this Irish borough from 1729 to 1852; but Waterford's finest period began just after 1780, somewhat too late for the affluent of the pre-revolutionary period to have taken much interest in them.

****

GUNS

****

Q. Where did these old guns come from and what kind are they?

A. This question comes daily in the Great Hall of the Governor's Palace where, according to an old record, the walnut-paneled walls were "decorated with guns and swords arranged in ingenious contrivances".

These are old English flintlock (or Brown Bess) muskets of the type used by both English and American troops in the Revolution and earlier. The particular collection at the Palace is from the Tower of London. They are in good working order, being tenderly cared for on regular schedule to keep them so.

They are, for you my gentlemen readers who may know what Felicity is talking about (for, oh shame to admit, she is not always sure she knows herself) 75 caliber, smooth bore, weighing between eleven and twelve pounds each and required thirteen separate formal loading and firing actions to get off a single shot. In a free firing situation, a British Regular was required to become so proficient with this weapon, he could fire four times a minute.

Although rifles were made as early as the 15th century (and even used as a military weapon in Scandanavia and Germany), they were brought to the colonies by Swiss and German settlers by the 1730's. They were first used as a military weapon in America during the Revolution. Although more accurate than a musket, they were, however, even more complicated to load since there was a patch around the ball and ramrodding was even more difficult and required greater time than the musket.

Long fowling pieces (like the one measuring 81 inches seen in the Brush-Everard House) had been used in Europe for ages. These were cumbersome weapons generally requiring a stationary position. They were most often propped on a unipod and used to shoot ducks and geese from a protective blind. Shorter fowlers were used for deer and other animals. These could be handled by the individual tracking his foe. Fowlers were more accurate because the long barrels held larger amounts of pellets or shot, the pressure upon firing was greater which resulted in better "keeping a pattern". In other words, the shot more often hit the mark since it went more often where it was supposed to go. Isn't this smashingly interesting?

The rifle probably was introduced into the colonies by Germanic-descent Pennsylvanians before mid-18th century and were made later in Kentucky and Virginia. The historic firearms buff will recall how much American rifle fire British soldiers swallowed in many important strategic skirmishes and Revolutionary battles.

****

GUNPOWDER

****

Those with great interest in firearms are commended to the experts (the master gunsmith or the gentlemen at the Powder Magazine). The latter mentioned indicate, however, the question they are most often asked is:

Q. Why did the British steal the gunpowder from the Magazine that night in April of 1775?

A. Ah, what an intelligent question! The answer is that the unpopular, if astute British Governor Dunmore, suspected (quite correctly) he was not as welcome in Virginia as he would choose to be. He feared for his safety and that of his family in those troubled times when events were reaching an obviously explosive stage. Indeed, there had been quite an explosion only the day before outside Boston. (You see there! Felicity is familiar with history elsewhere.) However, the news of the Lexington-Concord affair had not reached the Virginians. They were so enraged at Lord Dunmore's arbitrary order to remove the colony's powder, violence broke out in the night when the British Regulars were discovered. It was only because a highly respected and calmer citizen, Peyton Randolph—soon to become President of the First Continental Congress—prevailed upon the mob to wait until reason controlled action that there was not a second shot heard fired around the world that very night.

Later, the Governor was "persuaded", upon receiving intelligence that Patrick Henry and a large number of armed volunteers were marching on Williamsburg, that he should send a messenger ahead to meet them and pay for the powder rather than confront the determined men headed for his residence. While not completely placated, the firey orator's men had won a moral victory without bloodshed. The men returned to their homes and were elated when His Lordship and family quietly took leave of the Palace in the middle of the night some two months later and boarded a British ship lying at anchor in York River. Thus, despite all Dunmore's attempts to continue to govern by what might be termed "remote control", he was too remote to control. The patriots, upon the collapse of the Royal Government, seriously continued their business in the prelude to independence.

****

GUTTERS

****

Q. Why didn't they have them?

A. Gutters were not rare in England; but they were made of lead usually, and lead was just too expensive to import for this purpose, for which same reason you see few slate roofs.

There have been found a few partial remainders of what were obviously wooden gutters; but the impracticality of the necessary frequent replacement of rotting wooden gutters explains why they, too, were rare.

The problem of water run-off was solved generally with brick gutters laid at the building foundation. Less expensive, if less effective, was a single row of brick placed on the ground around the building. This was known as a "brick drip". Foundation walls of brick buildings were very thick—often two feet or more. At a point about three feet above the ground level where the brickwork would become somewhat thinner, there is a curved brick demarcation line known architecturally as the "water table". The very thick lower section, of course, provided structural strength; however, it served the additional purpose of dispersing the water running down a building's walls during a rain.

****

HENRY, PATRICK
(Also see GUNPOWDER)

****

Q. Why don't you mention his "Liberty or Death" speech?

A. It is mentioned when time permits; but the truth is, he did not make it here in Williamsburg. Henry's first famous speech as a legislator electrified the House of Burgesses in May, 1765. He was an unknown back-country lawyer, only twenty-nine years old and less than two weeks a member of the House of Burgesses. At that time, he was considered a crude upstart to many of his more conservative (and genteel mannered) constituents.

Historically, this speech is referred to as his "Treason" or "Caesar-Brutus" speech and was a magnificently vocal explosion against the hated British Stamp Act. The result, though frowned upon at the time by many who cried "Treason", later was said to have set the ball of revolution in motion.

Henry had kept the ball rolling in Virginia for ten years when he called upon the gentlemen of the Virginia Convention meeting March 23, 1775 (in the still standing St. John's Church in Richmond) to arm and prepare for war. There is NO complete and accurate account of the entire speech; but enough members who heard it remembered the few stirring words every American school child memorizes well enough.

Note: Felicity has, of late been alarmed due to a relatively new question no small number of visitors ask.

Q. Why was Patrick Henry hanged or shot?

A. Heaven forbid, dear reader; for we know, of course, he was not! He served as Virginia's first governor and four other terms, declining a sixth one. He was intermittently a member of the Virginia Legislature for years and remained "the reigning political Prince of Virginia" until his death in 1799.

Q. Why wasn't he ever President or something?

A. He didn't want to be. He declined one federal office after another as he practiced law and politics in Virginia and minded his "little flock" which numbered seventeen children, the youngest of whom was a 14-month-old son, when he died at the age of 63.

Note: About this matter of "hanging" or "shooting", we fear the firey orator has been confused with some other historical figure being depicted while those who ask this question were inaccurately viewing a television program; or, conversely and even more likely, viewing an inaccurate television program.

HORNBOOK

People do not ask this question; but if they pick up this little volume, they may. A hornbook is an ancient teaching aid. Originally, they were a leaf or page containing the alphabet, religious materials, etc. and were covered with a sheet of transparent horn and fixed in a frame with a handle. Now, a hornbook is a primer or a book of rudiments. This makes it abundantly clear why this one is so noticeably non-intellectual. Regretfully.

HOLES

Q. What are the holes we see in buildings where a brick is missing?

A. These are termed " putlock" and were left deliberately during construction, some experts believe, as a convenience. They were places to anchor horizontal scaffolding during masonry work which would, from time to time, require repair. If the holes were still there, the whole unpleasant business was rendered less tedious. This sounds logical; however, it must be admitted some other experts conjecture upon the indifferent habits of certain 18th-century brick masons. In either case, it is noted that many 20th-century birds are fond of them, often building nests within their shelter. And, Felicity once noticed a modern resident of this city industriously placing one apple and a sprig of holly in each hole on the front of his home (and this took some doing) to decorate for the Christmas season.

HOUSES

Q. Do people (or not unrarely, do "real" people) live in the houses which are not open to the public?

A. Indeed they do; and they ARE real people even though some emerging from them so curiously clad may appear to be ghosts of the past. Occupants of non-exhibited houses (and smaller dependency buildings behind or near them) generally are officials and employees of Colonial Williamsburg and pay rent to the Foundation. This is not to say that all employees live in the restored area for many own their own homes or rent elsewhere. Indeed, many who work here live in other towns and must commute just as some of you, dear readers, probably do.

A few houses are yet occupied by "life tenants" which is another matter of intense interest to the guests and will, therefore, be explained as a testimony to Mr. Rockefeller's concern for and interest in the inhabitants of the town at the time of his decision to restore it.

The purchasing of properties began in the late 1920's during the "big depression". Most people living here were happy to picture the town as it had appeared in the days of former glory. They accepted generous sale offers for their property which enabled them to build or rent elsewhere outside the confines of the original village. Others, some of whom were descendants of original owners, understandably were reluctant to leave their ancestral homes. To these, Mr. Rockefeller offered a happy solution. If they sold, the houses and grounds were restored to the original 18th-century appearance. Then, all maintenance and upkeep is provided while the former owners continue to live in them (rent and tax free) for the duration of their lives—hence the term, "life tenant". Further generous arrangement was made for dependants of these tenants who are granted a most adequate period of time to make decisions for living elsewhere after the life tenant's demise.

It is not difficult to understand that this was a particularly attractive arrangement for numerous residents living in old houses which were difficult to maintain properly during the depression. They were relieved of many burdens and much expense while they continued to enjoy their beloved family homes.

There are a few privately owned properties in the restored area today. There is no pressure, other than the offer of substantial purchase prices, placed upon the owners. Indeed, anything else would be completely contrary to the aims and purposes of the Foundation.

Note: As pleasant as it may appear to the guests to live in the restored area, it should be remembered that for the sake of authenticity in your experience of reliving the past here, numerous restrictions are endured by these occupants. For instance, you will note that the Duke of Gloucester Street is closed to modern traffic most of the time. Television antennas, air conditioners and other trappings of the 20th century must be hidden from public view. And, it should be noted that for the occupants to remain somewhat hidden from public view themselves, it is necessary to keep blinds drawn and doors latched. The visitor, of course, cannot know these houses are occupied by people who go about the daily task of living in a modern world within 18th-century surroundings.

A small plaque near the door designating "Private Residence" indicates those buildings in which you may find yourself a somewhat uncomfortable guest to have inadvertently entered a stranger's home.

****

INFORMATION

****

Q. Where do the guides get their information?

A. The Foundation has a Research Department, retaining several professional historians who are authorities in their various fields; and the results of their prodigious knowledge is forwarded through numerous channels to a Training Department consisting of three full-time Supervisor-Teachers.

Initially, before an employee is assigned to the first building he or she is to interpret, there is a period of several weeks of intensive study, the text materials for which cannot be carried to one's automobile in less than three trips. In addition, the Departments of Architecture, Collections and Gardens provide experts who lecture and give "on the scene" demonstrations in matters of their particular specialty.

An employee then remains in a continuous in-service training program as long as he or she is with the Foundation. The sessions (held during winter months) include daily classes, field trips to other historic areas and seminar research reports. The result is an appreciable knowledge of all aspects of the colonial period as Felicity hopes is noticeable.

Note: Although it may be difficult for the visitors to believe, after hearing such lengthy discourses regarding Virginia's past, the interpreters here DO know there were twelve other original colonies, all of which had their own patriot-leaders. Guides here study about these, too; but, alas, there is so little time to mention them.

Frequent comment is made regarding confusion upon seeing the same Hostesses or Hosts in different buildings on different days. The regular Hostess is trained to interpret ten different exhibition buildings (appropriately excluding the Gaol and Powder Magazine) and many are trained for garden and furniture tours. Hosts are seen at the Capitol, Wren Building and Carter's Grove Plantation. Guides interpreting the Gaol and Powder Magazine come under a different department and are active participants of the Militia as are many of the craftsmen.

This diversity of interpretive locations has the multi-purposed result of enhancing the employee's value to the Foundation. It renders scheduling more flexible, provides the guests' questions a ready answer regardless of where they ask (USUALLY, HOPEFULLY) and renders boredom practically nil.

Craftsmen work under the apprentice system which is being preserved here as are the crafts themselves. Master craftsmen train apprentices and journeymen as well as those employees who may be competent to interpret a craft even though they may not be skilled in the art of performing it.

We are happy to add that although an employee cannot answer every question asked, the usual result of inability to do so is an immediate recourse to the information source in order that the answer may be provided the guest while he is still present—or, at least, be known for the next person who may inquire into the subject.

****

INVENTORIES
(Also see PRICES)

****

Q. Why did they keep so many inventories and where do you get them?

A. Felicity ventures to suggest that our forefathers were not so spoiled as moderns and considered material possessions with enormous pride and of greater importance and value. Then, too, they were meticulous record keepers by nature as is evidenced in diaries, journals and account books kept by almost anyone of consequence.

However, there are two other quite practical reasons for inventories. They often accompanied fire insurance policies (this having been developed in Germany by the 15th century and companies established in America in the late 1700's). And, generally, an inventory was filed with a will probated in the courts in order to protect the executors. They are found, then, in old court records, family collections and often in rare document sections of libraries.

It is most fortunate for those moderns, whose profession it is to accurately reconstruct and refurnish the past, that our ancestors were so inclined and conveniently left these useful records of possessions and their value at that time.

****

IRONING

****

Please, patient reader, see CLOSETS even though you may find it somewhat frustrating that this subject is treated under that heading.

****

JAMESTOWN AND YORKTOWN
(Also see FOOD—please do not be distressed)

****

Q. How far is it to?

A. As the Cardinal flies (Felicity wishes to honor the state bird), it is approximately six miles to Jamestown. If one drives the scenic Colonial Parkway, it is slightly more but so rewarding. With the majestic James River on one's left and the unspoiled woods, abounding in much of Virginia's most beautiful indigenous trees and plants, the experience is unforgettable. The eye may catch an occasional glimpse of deer bounding through the forest or calmly watching you as you pass by. Bird watchers will enjoy the abundance of these feathered creatures, especially those whose habitats are about the water.

A return to Williamsburg via State Route 31 provides the visitor with other fascinating, if more modern, places to browse, and perchance acquire something he has long wanted.

Q. What is there to see at Jamestown?

A. The site of the early town of the first permanent English settlement in America has been excavated and one can traverse narrow dirt streets, exercising the imagination as to how the village looked over 350 years ago (with the aid of artists' conjectural paintings). There are artifacts and a museum in the official U. S. Park Service Information Center where there is an orientation film offered at regular intervals in the comfortable theater. Partial remains of a 17th-century brick church and churchyard still exist.

The original fort location probably was long since swallowed by the ever changing river. However, Jamestown Festival Park (administered by the Jamestown Corporation) is located just about one half mile away. Here, can be seen a reconstruction of the original fort, the three tiny ships which brought the first settlers across the ocean and an indian lodge which are interpreted by costumed guides in 17th-century dress. The Old and New World Pavillions (museums of prodigious interest to those re-living the past) and eating facilities along with other features of visitor interest are a part of The Festival Park.

Q. How far is it to Yorktown?

A. Approximately fourteen miles. This beautiful drive along the Colonial

Parkway provides the breathtaking view of the mighty river, York. Along the way, one passes the U.S. Naval Weapons Station. Here, from enormous loading docks, ships of our Atlantic fleet are supplied. And, before entering the historic little village where the decisive battle of the American Revolution was fought in October of 1781, one glimpses the fabulous Coleman Bridge spanning the river to connect with the Gloucester area opposite. This bridge is the longest double-swing span bridge in the United States!

Again, at Yorktown, the U.S. Park Service has provided an Information Center with museum and orientation film together with Park Service historians who can answer your questions. The Battlefield can be toured on foot or by car along well marked roads.

The quaint little village bears the charm of a bygone day with many original houses and interesting shops.

****

JEFFERSON, THOMAS

****

Q. How old was he when he wrote the Declaration of Independence?

A. Thirty-three, a lovely age—Felicity remembers it well. But most people express surprise that Mr. Jefferson was yet so young a man when he penned the document which marked us "Americans".

Young Jefferson, after attending the College of William and Mary where he studied Moral Philosophy, read law at the home of famed George Wythe. He was admitted to the bar in 1767 and was elected to the House of Burgesses in 1768 just in time to become involved in new struggles with England over the Townshend Duties and the resulting Non Importation Acts. In 1765, while still a student, he probably was standing in the Capitol outside the House of Burgesses hall and heard Patrick Henry deliver his famous "Treason Speech" against the Stamp Act.

It would appear many early influences in the village (the teen-aged Jefferson called "Devilsburg") planted seed which germinated quickly, flourished, and were full blown at the time America had need of his particular genius.

****

KINGS

****

Q. How many were there while Williamsburg was the Capital of Virginia?

A. Four; but kind reader, do not forget there were also Queens. As earlier stated, the Capitol moved from Jamestown in 1699. Queen Mary had died in 1694, leaving William III (her husband and Dutch cousin) to rule alone until his death in 1702; hence, the new Capital's name, Williamsburg. Queen Anne, Mary's surviving sister, was next in line for the throne and ruled (the last of the Protestant Stuarts) until her death in 1714. There followed, then George I, II and III, which last was on the throne at the time of the American Revolution. The Georges were of the German Hanoverian line; and the mention of this invariably brings up the next question.

Q. Why were German Kings ruling England?

A. This is complicated; but, alas, royalty usually is. As mentioned above, Queen Anne was the last Protestant Stuart; and England, in 1714, demanded a Protestant monarch. George I was the great grandson of James I whose daughter had married Frederick of Behemia. George I was Elector of Hanover; but both Stuart and Protestant blood flowed through his veins. British Parliamentary forces, nevertheless, were going the long (but seemingly only way) around to find their Protestant Stuart-blooded king.

George I cared little for England or its throne (but cared tremendously for his several mistresses). He did not speak English, conversing with English Ministers (when he did) in French, the recognized court language. He divorced his wife, Sophia Dorothea. All of this combined, made him something less than popular with his British subjects. George II, his son, while not filled with enthusiasm for the Empire he inherited, did have an enthusiastic wife, Catherine of Anspach, whose subtle influence furthered the ascendancy of Whig Minister Walpole. Walpole was good for England until ousted by the Prince of Wales (George II's own son) and his opposition forces in 1742. This all led up to the War of Austrian Succession in 1743 when George II led troops in person at Dettingen, the last time a British sovereign did this; and by 1746 the last Stuart uprising was surpressed.

When George II died in 1760, his grandson became George III (age 22) and reigned until his death in 1820 although a "mental malady", which touched him off and on many years, rendered him actually insane by 1810. In 1761, he had married Charlotte Sophia, Princess of Mecklinburg, which accounts for so many towns and counties in Virginia and North Carolina bearing those names. For the Carolinas were once part of Virginia as were seven other modern states carved from the enormous Virginia bounds after Independence. George III, despite his mental problems, seems to have been a model of domestic tranquility; but scandal touched his brothers and sons.

The present reigning House in England is descended from the Hanovarians, having changed the name to Windsor (for obvious reasons) at the time of the First World War.

Note: Felicity professes no great intellectualism in this above dissertation; but, rather, finds all this business of royalty as intriguing and confusing as must the reader.

****

KITCHENS

****

Q. Where are they?

A. Admittedly, on first thought, the answer to this would appear to be a great inconvenience. Kitchens in the southern colonies most often were located away from the house, to the side or back, and were separate buildings altogether. If one has spent a summer in the south, it will be clear that heat from tremendous fireplaces which, of necessity, burned from dawn 'till dark in the business of food preparation, was a factor. Another if less important reason, was the odors of cooking and burning wood which would permeate living quarters if kitchens were located therein.

Now, in our day when fireplace cooking has become a fad, we think this would add to the overall festivity. One's mind would change quickly, however, if his olfactory senses were subjected to continuous blending sniffs of boiling cabbage, frying fish, melting lard (not polyunsaturates, dear ladies, but hog fat), onions, leeks and other delicious things much to be enjoyed when set on the table. It would be quite a different matter if one had been smelling them cooking all day over open wood fires.

The other, and actually the most important reason for locating the kitchens some distance from the house, was the fire hazard. It was not uncommon for kitchens to catch fire several times a year. Obviously, building a new kitchen was cheaper than rebuilding an entire house.

The affluent planter's wife noted little inconvenience from the outside arrangement, she having servants who cooked, then carried the food (on the double, we might say) to the house and later returned all leftover food and dirty dishes from whence they came. Thus, the whole nasty business was out of sight and smell as it were. Females of the middlin' and poorer sort, having no servants, performed the task themselves. And, in this case, an assortment of daughters could be a great asset.

Note: Kitchen attendants in Williamsburg tell us the public views old kitchens with great delight, terming them "quaint". Curious cooking equipment of the past is a source of many questions; but the one everyone seems to ask is, "What is that big white cone-shaped thing on the table?" 'Tis a sugar loaf sweet reader. That product in granulated form, properly bagged and weighed, was not known to our ancestors.

****

LADIES

****

Q. Are all you ladies volunteers?

A. Heavens to Betsy, No! But, please refer to VOLUNTEERS for a more detailed, if less explosive answer.

Q. Did ladies stay in taverns?

A. Rarely, if ever. Please refer to TAVERNS and the reason will be made abundantly clear.

****

LECTURE

****

Q. Do we have to listen to a?

A. Of course not. Felicity adds, however, that it is absolutely necessary due to tremendous visitation, that most exhibition buildings are shown by group tours. The group number is dictated by the size and arrangement of each building. The visitor will understand, then, in order to eliminate absolute chaos, he must when requested, stay with a group. Whether he listens to the guide is entirely his own choice. And, most guides are painfully aware (albeit they bear the pain philosophically) of impressive numbers who simply turn off the audio (much the way we are prone to do when TV commercials are forced upon us) and rely exclusively upon the visual.

Felicity does, however, respectfully suggest that "turning off" an explanation is often but to cheat oneself. For unless one is extremely knowledgeable in the subject of colonial Virginia (which to learn more about is supposedly the reason he has come), he may take away only half an experience at best. This is not to imply that everything the guides say is of great import. For, 'tis a human failing (and admittedly a female one, and most especially when she enjoys a captive audience) to speak of "cabbages and kings and many things" at great length. The guides' vast storehouse of information (already discussed under that heading) often pours out in waves of astounding proportion. One thing leads to another until, like the pebble thrown into a pool, seemingly unending circles of conversation, chatter and critique eventually envelop the listener. The discerning guide, however, notes his or her enthusiasm has need of curbing when guests began to leave the tour in droves.

****

LINE

****

Q. Do we have to stand in it?

A. Alas, yes, when thou-art all here in such numbers as to create one. And, indeed, isn't it in the true tradition of the democratic process that he who comes first must be first served?

In the interest of truth, however, it is admitted there are occasions when certain individuals or parties are not required to stand in line. This, though, should not unduly upset the casual visitor who knows full well that royalty, heads of state, entertainers and other notables always enjoy slightly privileged procedures everywhere in the world.

Felicity has a happy suggestion for visitors standing in a long line while noting some special party has gone ahead of them (usually surrounded by a retinue of officials, security guards and the Press). The visitor obliged to wait briefly on such occasions often is privileged to be viewing some famous international personages. And, as an extra bonus in many cases, he may see himself on the evening news should his position in line have been in close proximity to TV cameras. Even some people waiting at the far end of a long line often are pleasantly surprised to find the camera has panned in briefly to register their somewhat remote reaction. Later, back home when relatives, employers and friends remark upon having seen them on a national network, it becomes a source of great personal pride.

In summary, lines in Williamsburg are (to make a most magnificent understatement) deeply regretted. They are, however, unavoidable as anyone living in the 20th century knows. And, if one did not find himself obliged to wait occasionally, he might begin to wonder if he could expect to see or hear anything worthwhile in the first place. Now, is that not logical?

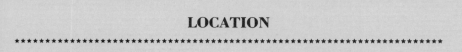

LOCATION

Q. When they reconstruct a building, how do they know for sure what had been there in the 18th century?

A. Such an intelligent question! And, the answer is as fascinating as it was valuable to those who found it necessary to know.

The most valuable record was a billeting map drawn by a French officer in 1781 showing where French troops were deployed about the town. It is now in the College of William and Mary Library. Streets, houses, shops, stores and even outbuildings were noted.

The Frenchman was not wrong. If he showed a cabinet shop (long gone by the 20th century), archaeologists find evidence that there had been such a shop on that location. Sketches, insurance policies, court property records, early photographs of original buildings and individual reminiscences of senior citizens who never forgot family stories passed down through generations also were worth their weight in reconstruction gold.

LONG

Q. How long does it take to go through here?

A. Oh, kind reader, permit us to abstain. 'Tis a question one cannot answer without qualification. Suffice it to say, each building (due to size limitation of groups or its historical importance) requires a different amount of time. And Felicity has already discussed the matter of it depending to some degree, partly, more or less, sometimes entirely, upon the interpreter. It is safe to suggest an approximate thirty minutes for more important buildings such as the Capitol, Palace or Wren Building and Carter's Grove Plantation; less for others and, of course, at one's own pace when not in a conducted tour situation.

LOOK LIKE

Q. How did they know what some of these old buildings which had disappeared look like?

A. One can visit the museum here and see the actual copperplate engraving, so called "The Bodleian" because it was found in that library at Oxford, England in 1929. It was made in Williamsburg about 1740 and shows views of the Governor's Palace, The Capitol and the College. And again, old drawings, descriptions in letters and diaries, personal reminiscences plus the early photographs of buildings which did last into the 19th century all aid the experts.

****

LUMBER

****

Q. Why do we see lumber and posts stacked around trees?

A. 'Twas a convenient way of air-drying small amounts of boards and fencing and was a common practice in colonial times.

****

MARBLE AND MARBLING

****

Q. Where did they get marble?

A. Accounts in the old VIRGINIA GAZETTES mention New England marble in 1768. A 1767 issue reports marble from Philadelphia had been shipped to the Accomac district of Virginia. There are mentions of marble in Amherst County in 1775 and quarries located there by 1779.

In the Governor's Palace, visitors see Italian, French, Belgian and Spanish marbles plus an example of one appropriately termed "Conglomerate". This is rare and usually seen on table tops. It came from an area between Italy and France where, millions of years ago, a geological earth "fault" fused the pink French and white Italian (and some other types) together, creating an interesting effect. It appears to be bits and pieces glued together; but is rather a "mutation" marble created by the convulsions of nature. The homes of the affluent planters often featured imported marbles.

Q. Why is part of the Capitol interior painted to look like marble?

A. Because it was that way in the 18th century. It was an art and fashion in England and some say feathers were used to create the interesting effect. The expense of importing or even transporting large amounts of marble for structural purposes rendered marbling in the colonies an economy measure while yet providing the appearance of elegance. Since it was so much in style in England, we assume the colonials thought economic deceit was admissable here. It was popular in the upper colonies also.

****

MATCHES

****

Q. Did they have them?

A. No, although attempts in the 18th century to cause ignition by use of chemicals resulted in a friction match devised by an Englishman, John Walker, in 1827. In colonial days, one was obliged to use methods of friction employing flint, tender, steel or the more primitive method of stick and groove. A sunglass was sometimes used. Needless to say, a fire once started, was respected if controlled and would, therefore, by banked carefully when not needed in order that tapers could be lit from smoldering embers later. This eliminated the necessity of starting all over again with one of the more difficult methods.

Another frequent question is in regard to curious iron stands or hanging pan-like contraptions. These were called "Betty Lamps" (Felicity does not know who Betty was). Their pans usually contained whale oil and a wick which would furnish some light and was a source for lighting tapers, the disagreeable smoke and odor notwithstanding.

Note: After some research and questioning experts in such matters, we find that the early Greeks and Romans used oil for lighting. The so called "Betty" lamp of England and the colonies, we are told, was named by a mutation of an adjective of the German language, "besser" (meaning better) —therefore, a better lamp—than something else they had been using. Supposedly. However, they were also referred to by another such shocking term, Felicity could not bring herself to pursue it. However, having mentioned it, she suspects some reader will. Therefore, she respectfully suggests the term had something to do with a earlier usage of the word with reference to "dirty". We do not think the latter term had the slightest thing to do with "Betty". Hopefully.

****

MATTRESSES
(Please see BEDS)

****

MAZE

Q. What is it and where is it?

A. Any maze is a puzzle, so to speak, where confusing trails with dead ends test the intelligence and/or luck of the individuals attempting to locate the exit.

One finds maze games printed in newspapers and in children's (how to keep them interested and out of trouble) books. The maze at the Governor's Palace is located to the left as one leaves through the rear door and beyond the walled formal gardens. One can go into it—physically, it being fashioned of living native American holly and copied from similar "deceits" known to be popular in European gardens of the time. 'Twas a frivolous diversion, appealing to both young and old; but is now most likely Williamsburg's greatest attraction for children.

Felicity divulges a secret which renders it more popular to weary modern parents. In effect, the maze becomes an excellent subsitute for a temporary baby-sitter. There is but one gate, serving as both entrance and exit. Due to the dense growth, there is no way to climb over, under, or squeeze through at any point within. There is a comfortable bench shaded by a wall near the entrance-exit. Sit then, tired mothers and harassed fathers, resting in the happy assurance that so long as your children do not come out, they are at least safely lost. For the moment.

Felicity hastens to mention one word of caution. Should parents become alarmed regarding an unusual extended period of time and their children still do not emerge, wait yet a little longer. For, it has been noted that youngsters find the exit in approximately half the time required by adults— even those with Doctorate degrees. And, oh sad to admit; but the record was set by "Lassie" during a filming visit here once!

****

MERCHANT'S SQUARE
(Please see AREA)

****

MIRRORS

****

Q. Why are mirrors often in several pieces?

A. First, dear reader, permit Felicity to tease. You will not hear the term "mirror" in exhibition buildings for 'twas not in usage at the time of our ancestors. Mirrors were "looking glasses", draperies were "curtains" or "hangings", and contractors (builders) were undertakers". Isn't that fun?

But to answer the question: About 1688, in France, an invention for casting glass led to the manufacturing of plate glass as we know it, the back coating then generally being a thin mixture of tin and mercury. Techincal limitation regarding the size a sheet of plate could be produced together with the high tax levied on plate glass in England, dictated the custom of fashioning larger looking glasses of several, sometimes numerous, pieces.

****

MONEY

****

We have yet to find a soul indifferent to the subject of money. For, indeed, it has figured prominently in the rise and fall of empires, marriage, reputations, politicians and artists of every sort (not to mention the stock markets) since man could not obtain the necessities of existence other than by its power. One of our favorite philosophers said something to the effect that money was a matter of such universal interest, be there a mere mention of it and every man is suddenly of the same religion!

For some historical understanding of "money" in 18th-century Virginia as opposed to it in the sense we think of it today (and, of course, most of us think more of it than have it), it is necessary to mention a current controversial subject in connection with it.

Hard money or real money, as such, was painfully scarce in colonial Virginia, albeit the colony was the largest and most affluent in America. The development of the tobacco economy, which was firm by mid-17th century, provided Virginia's money—the golden weed. To put it another way, tobacco paid the bills, either literally in it's physical form, or by the use of tobacco warehouse receipts or bills of exchange to an Agent and served much the same purpose as checks and bank drafts in our day.

By English law, Virginia tobacco was sold only to the mother country and was required to be delivered within English or American ships. It would leave the planters' wharves or public warehouses consigned to an "Agent" in England. This Agent firm handled the sale (naturally for its own profit) at the highest possible price. When sold, the planters' profit, if any, was entered in account books and the Agent would then assume the role of "personal shopper". He would purchase a long list of items (ranging from aprons to zinc) which had accompanied the tobacco shipment and send it on a return boat to the planter in payment for what Queen Elizabeth I had called Virginia's "bewitching vegetable".

This practice was known as the "mercantile system" where the colony existed for the benefit of the mother country—bartering raw materials in exchange for manufactured goods. Now, it becomes clear why the wealthier Virginians (because they had land and that land made tobacco) possessed English furniture, silver, tea, fabrics and the like. It is also how they obtained the fine Oriental niceties—carpets, fabrics, wallpapers and spices—came through the English trade.

Money which did circulate in the colony was more often of Spanish or French origin, brought in by sailors, sailing masters and other visitors. The resulting confusion associated with figuring relative value of this foreign currency to English and of that to the ever fluctuating price of tobacco was enough to create a few modern-type aches and pains associated with matters of money.

This subject is so fascinating, it leads the author to elaborate still further as is, admittedly, her custom by nature.

From mid-18th century to the Revolution, the lack of currency in Virginia confounded the growing problems with the mother country's new "hard-line" approach to policies concerning her American "children". New taxes levied in England were to be paid by the colonies in MONEY. Virginia had TOBACCO. Thus, it becomes clear why Virginians were among the first and most verbal in protest to new taxation policies. 'Tis a matter so complex, yet of such preeminence among the colonys' vexations from the French and Indian War until the Revolution, we sincerely hope the non-historian will pursue the subject in depth in some learned source.

To prove Felicity's impartial nature, she begs to inform the reader that the English merchants and agents making claims for tremendous debts owed them by many Virginia planters were often well founded. We do not wish to reopen any old wounds, however.

It may be of interest to modern visitors whose professions include the Church, public service, legislative or the like, to know that their colonial Virginia counterparts were even paid "by the weed". And it surprises some lawyers to learn that a very intense legal battle between the Virginia Anglican clergy and the House of Burgesses over the clerics' claim for "back weed" led to one of the most famous trials in the annals of American law. In his first important case, one Patrick Henry (self-taught attorney) in 1763, though losing his case, won a virtual victory. He set the stage for the argument of government by consent of, and for the common good of the governed which was used in various interpretations during the next thirteen years of American troubles with England.

The author hopes the reader has found the above exquisitely edifying.

She does, nonetheless with regret, return to the purpose of this little work which is to answer questions most often asked by visitors. She also notes that her propensity for reminding the reader of her purpose may arouse some doubts as to the validity of that purpose in the first place. However, in all good conscience and with great fun, she continues the subject of questions about money.

Q. How much has been spent on the Restoration?

A. Before he died in 1960, Mr. John D. Rockefeller, Jr. had spent well over 70 million dollars in restoration, reconstruction and related facilities. So conceived as a non-profit educational foundation, he knew the operational expense could never be met by conventional income. He therefore, further generously endowed Colonial Williamsburg with an additional trust fund of more than 50 million dollars which has been invested in securities (all of which are listed annually in the President's Report and is public information). The income from the endowment has been sufficient so far to make up the loss of over a million dollars a year.

Since their father's death, the Rockefeller brothers have contributed over 10 million dollars for necessary expansion programs (many of them for the greater convenience and pleasure of the guests). A recent bequest of 5 million dollars was made by the late Mrs. John D. Rockefeller, Jr. to the Foundation through her will.

Q. How can Colonial Williamsburg possibly lose over a million dollars a year?

A. To the incredulous individual among well over a million visitors a year, this is certainly a valid question. It is answered by the fact. Revenue from ticket sales is but a small drop in the proverbial bucket. The visitor must notice how much is offered without charge. There is the Information Center with its educational and entertainment program, bus service, open gardens and craft demonstrations, exhibits of the Folk Art Museum as well as the museum collection of artifacts. In addition, special programs such as Militia Musters with the Drum and Fife Corps, fireworks displays, Colonial Sports' Day, Field Music Day, competing Cricket teams and others, offer unique entertainment for everyone.

Other educational programs include The Antiques Forum, Garden Symposium, Williamsburg International Assembly, The Student Burgesses and a joint research center in conjunction with the College of William and Mary known as the Institute of Early American History. All of this adds up to an expenditure of staggering proportions for reasons of preserving the American heritage for the American people.

Q. Who owns Colonial Williamsburg then?

A. It owns itself. Mr. Rockefeller, when convinced it was being properly planned, executed and administered, gave it to itself. It is administered by a President and Vice Presidents, Directors, Assistant Directors and Supervisors of the divers departments (just as any large, complex organization) who are answerable to an unpaid official Board of Trustees composed of some of the most eminent individuals in the field of American business, education, the arts, and other prestigious professions.

Q. How much did (this or that) cost in the 18th century?

A. Alas, those answers which can be given are of little value due to a relatively modern term, "inflation". You, gentle reader, are so well acquainted with and painfully aware of the awesome effects of the term as to make it unnecessary to explain that a lapse of two hundred years renders comparison impossible.

Guides do not avoid the question. They merely answer relatively, it being their only choice. For instance, the most valuable possession listed in the 1744 will of gunsmith James Geddy, Sr. was one Negro boy named Jack, valued at 30 pounds. Now, 30 pounds was approximately one third the annual salary of a Professor of Philosophy at the College.

Then Thomas Jefferson once suggested a minimum list of 148 titles in 379 volumes for a non-too-scholarly brother-in-law's library. In plain bindings this modest collection would cost about 107 pounds and twice that if done in leather by a famous German binder, Mr. Jefferson added. At today's rate, does it not pain you, kind reader, to think of how few of Felicity's little work could be purchased with a like sum? She concludes philosophically, however it could never snuggle on a shelf with Homer, Dryden, Milton and Shakespeare regardless of its cover.

You will find some discussion of this aspect of colonial prices again under TAVERNS and SHOES.

****

MORTAR
****

Q. What did they use for mortar?

A. Lime and sand. Lime was plentiful, a readily available source bordering Virginia shores in billions of oyster shells to be had for the taking. However, their mortar made sans later cement, was less durable and unpossessed of the property of "setting" under water and was not used as extensively as today's cement mortars.

****

MUSIC AND MUSICAL INSTRUMENTS
****

Felicity is happy to say that there is an 18th-century music master's shop in Williamsburg. Since it is rare to find a human who does not like music in one form or another, it is a prodigiously popular place. In the shop can be seen and heard the instruments and music of that period. The author commends the reader of more than passing interest to address all technical questions to those who are qualified to answer them. And if one is only passing and has not interest, he will most likely find it once he enters the shop.

Included here are three most frequently musical questions asked in the building of greatest volume visitation, the Governor's Palace.

Q. What is a harpsichord?

A. A musical instrument resembling our baby grand piano although longer and thinner and has a keyboard or double keyboard, the strings of which are plucked by a quill or jack rather than struck with a hammer as a piano is. They originated in the 14th century and were very popular instruments for fine music until superseded by the piano in the 19th century. One will note this popularity has enjoyed a recent happy revival.

Q. What were some of the other most popular instruments?

A. The violin (if you were conversing with Mr. Jefferson, the "fiddle" if 'twer Mr. Henry, both of whom played them expertly, if differently), cello, flute and the oboe to mention a few one would have heard in the ballroom during a musical.

Q. Who were the most popular composers our forefathers would have enjoyed here?

A. Many, of course; but we are reasonably certain the British Governors and their guests would have musical tastes including large portions of Handel, Mozart, Corelli and Schütz. However, as mentioned under DANCING, (when things became lively) old ballads, jigs and airs known for generations would certainly echo through the rooms.

****

NO-NO'S

****

Q. May we sit down (smoke, etc., etc.)?

A. Gentle reader, the answer is . . . oh, dreadful pain to put it down . . . but,

PLEASE NOTE: Of course, Williamsburg ladies do not throw little boys (or even big ones) from chairs. Neither do they slap hands when guests fondle priceless fabrics, wall coverings and other objects. It is requested that all visitors, regardless of age, sex or size, refrain from sitting or touching unless invited to do so. The gentlemen (and ladies inclined to the habit) will be pleased to find large urns conspicuously awaiting cigarettes and cigars outside the exhibition buildings. The necessity for such safety measures is so simple as to render it unnecessary to mention it. Naturally.

"no"—that is unless you are invited to do so, which in the case of smoking you will never be. Albeit this is in no way connected with a modern controversy, but is merely a sensible safety rule. Danger to irreplacable historic buildings, priceless antiques and close proximity to other people renders the habit (admittedly popularized by Virginians) distrusted of the consequences within exhibition buildings and shops. 'Tis not necessary to elaborate on what would happen to antique furniture, fabrics, wall coverings, books and the like if touched, handled and sat upon over a million times a year.

****

ORIGINAL

****

Q. Is this house original or has it been restored?

A. Yes. Oh, dear Felicity is thinking like a female again! She means if the house is restored, it IS original. The terms original, restored, and reconstructed are all quite confusing. The subject is quickly rendered elementary.

An original building obviously has been here all along. Over decades, buildings change as owners make additions, removals and include new conveniences. Restoration of an original building then is the art (and an art it is) of taking it back to its proper appearance in terms of time. It is, in a sense, a process of "demodernizing". Buildings undergoing restoration are subjected to a certain indignity in that they are quite literally "stripped to the bare bone" and examined from every possible angle. When all conditions are satisfied, they are put back together again like Humpty Dumpty would like to have been (Felicity added that for the wee ones) and spruced up with paint of the original color. (See PAINTS for further discussion).

Reconstructed buildings, on the other hand, are rebuilt completely (usually on their original foundations) to look just as they appeared in colonial days. This requires enormous skill and knowledge and is the business of specialists in the matter of reconstructing the past.

****

OWNERS OF COLONIAL WILLIAMSBURG
Please see discussions under HOUSES and MONEY.

****

****

OYSTER SHELLS
(Also see MORTAR)

****

Q. Why are there so many piles of oyster shells lying around?

A. They were, as stated earlier, a prodigious available source of lime used to make mortar, plaster, soap, whitewash and other bleachers. Lime was used in the process of tanning leather and has long been known to counteract acidity in soil. And in Tidewater Virginia, crushed oyster shells were a frequently used material for paving walks as is much in evidence here today.

****

PAINT

****

Q. Is this Williamsburg blue?

A. Yes and No. Oh, dear. Felicity is doing it again. What we mean is that there is really no such thing. Let us put it this way. A number of shades of blue are seen in Williamsburg; but that is because they were typical of the period and the colors are those obtained from natural pigments. Paint generally was shipped in from England; therefore, Williamsburg colors are typical of the fashionables hues of those "at home" at that time.

Five major colors predominated in pre-revolutionary Virginia: greens, blues, greys and various shades of buff and gold, and (less often) red. There were two main sources of obtaining pigments—from mineral or inorganic colors and from natural dyes. White pigments were available in white lead or zinc; yellows in lead chromes and zinc chromate; green in chrome oxide, green earth and copper; blue in potash and cobalt; blacks of varying degrees in carbon and lamp blacks; and reds in oxides of iron or red lead. They mixed pigments with oil or water depending on where and how they were to be used.

The term "Williamsburg blue", to return to the question, has become commercially popular over the years as modern paint companies are reproducing as faithfully as possible, many of the colors used in Williamsburg. The Foundation's own experts mix the paints here to match perfectly those found on original buildings and woodwork.

Q. How do they know what those original colors were if a house has been repainted numerous times?

A. Here we have the experts again. Meticulous chipping and very patient removal by rubbing ever so gently with a solvent, layer upon layer, will be rewarded by the appearance of the original color. When done by an expert!

Q. Why are most interior walls painted white?

A. There were two very practical reasons. Paint was outrageously expensive to begin with and England also placed a tax on it. Remember what was said in the discussion of money and why Virginians were so hasty in their protests to taxation, particularly when levied on items they were forced to buy from the mother country? This made painting of no small expense. The other reason is that white walls reflected candlelight, a thought which would seldom occur to moderns.

In fact, anything which reflected light—metals, glass, hurricane globes (which also kept drafts from snuffing the candle flame) were used to increase "candle power". And thinking in terms of the housewife, muse upon how quickly walls would become dirty in those days with lighting by candles and heating by fireplaces. Whitewashed walls, then, were cheaper than repainting; for this distasteful project was repeated several times a year if one found dirty walls distasteful.

Q. Why did they paint wood paneling so much?

A. In our day, when wood paneling is very expensive and wood grains have a particular appeal, this does seem ridiculous. But to our ancestors (and particularly in the English fashion-following Virginia stronghold) only "finer" woods would have been left natural with but oil and polished finish. Thus, most paneling which is not painted here is black walnut, a plentiful wood at that time. Pine was exceedingly plentiful but considered inferior in grain detail to walnut or oak and was, therefore, almost always painted. You see only one rare example of oak paneling in Williamsburg and that in a small bedroom at the Peyton Randolph House. It is not that oak was not abundant; but that England had need of it for building ships for her navy.

* *

PALACE

* *

Q. How many governors lived here?

A. The hostess will quickly answer, "Nine—seven English governors and two governors of the Commonwealth of Virginia." Then the visitor will ask.

Q. Who were they?

A. The hostess will then less quickly, reply: "Governor Spotswood who built it" (pause) "then Governor Drysdale" (pause) "Gooch" . . . (longer pause) "and, oh, yes, Governor Dinwiddie. I remember him because he became very unpopular with the people. Then, there were Governors Fauquier, Boutetourt and Dunmore; and, of course, Patrick Henry and Thomas Jefferson."

Q. Did the Palace just have three bedrooms?

A. No, it had (and has) eleven. The third floor where there are eight, cannot be shown to the public because of the narrow spiral stairway leading to it. This will be discussed under STAIRWAYS.

Q. Why did it burn?

A. Kind reader, please see FIRES for Felicity is weary and this is covered under that heading.

****

PEWTER
****

Q. What is it?

A. Pewter is sometimes called the "poor man's silver" although today, it is highly prized, being lead free, easy to care for, and still less expensive than silver while yet looking elegant. The alloy's principal ingredient is tin with various other added materials. Early pewter contained large amounts of lead, giving it the bluish tinge and increased malleability. It could, however, cause lead poisoning if one ate or drank from pewter containers with too high a lead content. Antimony, copper, busmuth and zinc are other materials included.

Because of its relatively small intrinsic value in the 17th and 18th centuries, pewter (like our every-day dishes) was not carefully preserved. Antique pewter collecting, therefore, is a delightfully expensive hobby should hubby be happily generous toward financing such a diversion.

Collecting early American pewter is even more exciting and expensive because it is yet more scarce than English or Continental and much more difficult to identify. Much early pewter made in the colonies was melted down from damaged or worn imported pieces and refashioned into some useful vessel or utensil by traveling tinkers. (Felicity is charmed by that term.) These versatile itinerate craftsmen were concerned primarily with making a living and had little interest in leaving a "touch" or marker's mark on their wares.

Williamsburg visitors are delighted to witness craftsmen making beautiful silver and brass pieces and address many questions to the artisans who perform the tasks. Pewter is listed here simply because the public appears to be less familiar with it than other metals; and because fine pewter is produced locally and is available on Merchant's Square and in the restored area.

****

POLISH

****

Q. What do they use to polish the silver, brass, pewter etc.?

A. Oh, dear, 'tis not our purpose to become commercial; albeit we understand why, noting all the gleaming, this questions is asked so frequently by the female visitor. Felicity is not being facetious when she answers, "mostly elbow grease"; for that is an old term for the physical action of polishing. A lot of it is necessary and, of course, there are numerous people here whose job is to do just that. And they do a brilliant job if it, do they not?

As for the polishes used, they are obtainable in modern markets and shops and generally contain ingredients used (blended one way or another) centuries ago: pumice, tripoli and jewler's rouge.

****

POPULATION

****

Q. What is the population of Williamsburg?

A. According to the Chamber of Commerce, it is approximately 10,000 within the city limits. What is termed "the greater Williamsburg area", that served by the business community, approaches 35,000.

Q. What was it in the 18th century?

A. Never more than 2,000 except during Publick Times when the temporary influx of people concerned with business, politics and pleasure, bloated the little village with an additional two to four thousand.

****

PEOPLE
(Also see SERVANTS and SLAVES)

****

Q. Where did the poor people live in the 18th century?

A. Williamsburg had few poor people as we think of the term. Slaves and indentured servants, apprentices and the like generally lived with masters or employers as stated earlier. Williamsburg was largely what we would term "middle class', made up of craftsmen, merchants, civil servants and professionals such as physicians, apothecaries (who often considered themselves physicians), teachers and clerics. Some affluent planters owned houses in town and some of the upper class (Randolphs, Wythes, and the Governor, of course) lived here the year 'round.

The truly indigent were relatively rare and when present, either were kindly tolerated and aided by the more responsible of the privileged class or, otherwise, run out of town by the less tolerant and less privileged.

To expand into the vast colony, the small farmer (whom we might think of as poor) was far more numerous in colonial Virginia than most people realize. Nor, was he really poor. He lived simply and worked hard as did his entire family. But as a "freeman" (a property holder), he could hold his head high. To him, this was a "richness" scarcely comprehensible to most moderns living in our age of fantastic economic complexity. Felicity thinks 'tis a subject to ponder; for the pride of "owning" something runs deep in our heritage and philosophy and, in part, makes us what we are.

Q. How many people come here each year?

A. Oh, my—we grow and grow. 'Tis now well over a million.

****

PORCELAIN
(See CERAMICS)

****

****

PRICES
(See MONEY, TAVERNS and SHOES)

****

QUEENS
(See KINGS

****

RECONSTRUCTED AND RESTORED
(See ORIGINAL)

****

RESTROOMS

****

Q. Where is a?

A. Now, this indeed, is a frequent and necessary question; for, in Williamsburg, things are not always what they appear to be. And, although public facilities are provided and designated as such, they are seldom where or look like what one might expect. Authentically, however, one finds them not within, but without, the exhibition buildings. In the restored area, look for former dependencies (outbuildings of all kinds—laundries, smoke houses, garden houses etc.) where you may observe 20th-century ladies and their daughters emerging from one side and 20th-century gentlemen and their sons from the other. This is an excellent indication the building is now a public restroom.

All modern service facilities are equipped, of course, in the conventional manner.

****

RUGS

****

Q. Wouldn't they have had rugs on the floors?

A. Those who could afford to, certainly; and you see them. The wealthy owned fine Oriental and English carpets. Often, industrious genteel ladies fashioned elegant ones of needlepoint. Some woven carpeting is to be seen.

The visitor asking this question, usually is standing in a room without one —which is why the room is without one—because the visitors are permitted to walk through that room. Priceless antique carpets cannot be abused anymore than priceless furnishings, fabrics and wall hangings. Hence, where the traffic patterns in exhibition buildings permit moderns to move about, the lack of a carpet or rug is another "judicious compromise".

****

SCREENS
(Also see FIREPLACES)

****

Q. What are those little standing screens in front of fireplaces?

A. These are adjustable "pole screens" (usually embellished with needlework) which could be moved about and the screen section moved up and down on the pole in order to deflect intense heat from the body when one was seated near an open fire.

Q. Didn't they have window screens back then?

A. No. They lived insectually. Sorry! Felicity loves to "coin" words even though the dictionary is so full of better ones.

****

SHINGLES

****

Q. Are the shingles made of wood?

A. The Governor's Palace was the only building in 18th-century Williamsburg with a slate roof. Most houses and even the Capitol were covered with wooden shingles, sometimes called shakes. Cypress and cedar were the woods most often used. They were made by hand with the use of a "draw knife" and were secured by means of wooden pegs. A shingle maker demonstrates this ancient craft here. Expertly.

Shingles on reconstructed and restored houses today (except the Palace which is slate) resemble the old wooden ones so much they are thought of as "magnificent deceptions". Especially made for Colonial Williamsburg, they are a combination of cement and other materials, are fireproof and extremely heavy. Many guests express a desire to use them on new homes under construction until made aware of the expense involved, at which time most consider compromise.

★★★

SHOES

★★★

Q. How long would it take a shoemaker to make a pair?

A. In a typical 18th-century twelve-hour day, a good craftsman could complete one or two pairs depending on utility or elegance of style.

Q. How much would a pair of shoes cost back then?

A. Roughly from 4½ to 8 shillings a pair, again depending on utility or elegance. Today, a shilling might buy a good pair of shoe laces which proves the earlier expressed theory that relative prices of things then and now is relatively unrelevant.

Q. Are these iron bars set between the short iron posts outside doorways for scraping mud from shoes and boots?

A. Yes. And, wouldn't it be nice if the custom were revived—especially in households where there are little boys who play in the mud and husbands who "forget" to wipe their feet before entering?

★★★

SHUTTERS

★★★

Q. Why are the wide wooden shutters inside brick buildings?

A. Ah, we must again point out the particular attention paid to real craftsmanship in the old days. It was a style borrowed from "home". Brick buildings had very thick solid brick walls for purposes of strength and insulation and left sufficient space for window seats and interior shutters or blinds which were fashioned to fold back and become part of the woodwork. We mentioned this briefly when explaining why most brick buildings were embellished with some decorative arrangement around windows and doors on the exterior.

****

SIZE OF PEOPLE
Please see BEDS. Oh, dear, we ARE sorry it comes under that subject!
****

SLAVES AND SERVANTS
(Also see BEDROOMS and POOR PEOPLE)
****

Q. How many slaves (or servants) would they have had?

A. This question is asked everywhere. It would depend upon the financial status of those who owned any at all, of course. For instance, Mr. James Geddy, Sr. (a gunsmith) owned three; Mr. Everard, once a mayor of Williamsburg, perhaps five; and a wealthy planter, perhaps as many as eighty to one hundred. There were a few extremely affluent planters who may have had even more, deploying their services on several plantations.

Permit us to explain the term "indentured servant". Many people, some well educated, were too poor to pay passage and move to the new world yet wanted to come very badly. They would contract to sell their labor for a specified number of years, depending on the individual's skill and usefulness and upon the size of his family which must be transported. Thus, passage was paid through the planter's pocketbook. At the end of the indenture period, the contract was satisfied and the "indentured" was given (according to law) fifty acres of land. He was then a "freeholder" and had the rights and privileges of voting and holding office just as anyone else. Many fine people who made excellent responsible citizens started out in the new world in just this way.

In fact, the first Negroes in America came as indentured servants aboard a Dutch trading ship in 1619. The development of the institution of slavery came about due to a labor shortage for the cultivation of tobacco which had become Virginia's economy by 1640. Indentures for blacks were increased by law until, finally by 1660, it was virtually life-time servitude, or outright slavery. Human beings, somewhere, were willing to sell other human beings to slave-ship captains who were more than willing to transport and sell them to planters, some of whom recognized and worried about the evil and some of whom (in another age) thought nothing of it.

Patriots and enlightened men of the 18th century (one, being Thomas Jefferson) were as firmly entrapped in the system as was the slave himself. These men fought to eradicate the system but failed. After the Revolution, they were responsible (men from many colonies) for legislation which out-

- 83 -

lawed the slave trade and permitted private manumission (freeing of slaves). Legislation failed, however, in spite of all efforts, to abolish the system entirely; and it is a sad fact of history that this issue was not settled until a century after the Revolution.

****

SOAP

****

Q. What did they use for soap?

A. Well, certainly not the kind everyone wishes everyone else would. (Felicity could not control herself here). But to answer the question, soap was known in England in the 14th century and there is reference to this "product" as early as the 1st century when Pliny described it being used by Germanic tribes. In England, from 1712 to 1853, there was a heavy tax on soap. The colonists generally made their own.

Fats and oils were combined with lye, obtained by leaching wood ashes or oyster shells, and were all boiled together in a large vessel. This could be colored or scented slightly if desired. Soap usually was moulded in a ball shape. Under the topic of "Bathing", it was pointed out that soap did not disappear as quickly then as now. In one respect, however, our ancestors had an advantage over us, never having been subjected to a single soap commerical.

****

STAY

****

Q. Where can we stay tonight?

A. The historic triangle (including Williamsburg, Jamestown and Yorktown (all connected by the Colonial Parkway) features more than forty motels and hotels and almost that number of private guest homes. There are several camping areas for travelers who enjoy their homes on wheels. The Williamsburg-James City County Chamber of Commerce provides information as well as a Travel and Reservations Desk at the Information Center of Colonial Williamsburg. Additionally, many local businesses, if unable to accommodate you themselves, kindly attempt to find a suitable place for you elsewhere.

STEPS AND STAIRWAYS

Q. What are the metal pieces set into stone steps?

A. These are "cramps" (iron pieces with bent ends) and were used to hold the stone securely in place. The unreliability of 18th-century mortar has been mentioned.

Q. Can we go up the spiral staircast (at the Palace)?

A. Oh, dear, "no". Really, this would just be out of the question. You see, it is not only too narrow for two bodies to pass (and you can see there are almost always more than two bodies passing around here); but 'twould make many visitors dizzy as well. It was used as a service stairway in the 18th century (albeit 'twas the only way to reach the third floor) and there is, to-day, truly nothing up there save the eight now unfurnished bedchambers. So, you can readily see, this request simply must be denied. Felicity is so sorry.

Q. Where does that awful little stairway which looks like a ladder go?

A. This is asked at the Brush-Everard House and always on the second floor before the guests have seen the back downstair's bedchamber the stairs lead to. Indeed, they are frightening in appearance and, no doubt, required no small amount of agility and courage to ascend or descend them. They were, nonetheless, another service stairway.

For your protection, a platform has been built over the top portion in order that you may look into the child's room without stepping down and up again on small triangular treads which divide and lead into both bed-chambers they serve. These little steps, being unseen, create a greater illusion to add to the ladder-like construction. It is doubted they were ever much in use.

Q. Didn't they carpet steps?

A. We find no reference to it here; however, "stair carpets" were made at the time. A Smithsonian Institute report notes that Mr. Jefferson ordered them for the White House. Due to the enormous expense of carpets, areas of great traffic such as halls and steps were left bare most often. But, references indicate "stair carpets" were made of a canvas-type material and often were painted or decorated by painted design.

****

TAVERNS

****

Q. Did ladies stay in them?

A. Rarely, if ever. It is possible that a wealthy planter and his wife and family, having need of temporary accommodations during times when there was little going on in the town, might have taken several rooms.

As mentioned earlier, the town became a thronging metropolis when the Government sat in the spring and fall and it was more than difficult for a man to find a place to rest his weary bones. Consequently, when business was booming, tavern owners often rented "bed room" (which being "room in a bed") and charged according to the number of unfortunate fellows obliged to share the same one. 'Twould be interesting to know if this "indelicate custom" (according to a French traveler in the colonial days) might not have originated the old expression, "Politics create strange bedfellows".

Q. Where did ladies stay then?

A. Of course, some wealthy families owned houses in town which eliminated the problem for them (and, no doubt, for many of their relatives and friends).

There are advertisements in the old VIRGINIA GAZETTES (usually placed by widows forced to the necessity of supporting themselves) indicating that they had spacious and airy rooms to let to genteel ladies on the first floor. Felicity wishes that advertisement read: To let to genteel ladies, spacious and airy rooms on the first floor. That has a more dignified ring to it, do you not think?

The other recourse for ladies who wished to enjoy the festivities in the Capital during Publick Times was to visit nearby plantations—again, the relatives or friends or friends of relatives, or relatives of friends. The colonial Virginians' custom of entertaining large numbers of house guests for extended periods is, to moderns, unbelievable. One example should suffice to convince the incredulous reader. A planter of no small financial, political and social consequence owned a nearby plantation. In a letter to his brother, he mentioned (with admirable restraint) "Our nephew and his wife left us this morning, having stopped by when on their honeymoon and liking it here so well, have tarried with us until their second child was weaned only last week".

Q. How much did it cost to spend the night?

A. This, of course, depended upon the fineness of the establishment just as rates vary today. One old existing Bill of Fare lists a York County tavern's prices in part, thusly:

A gentleman, with bed to himself when available . . . 7½ pence. It is interesting to note the charge for his horse was precisely the same. However, seemingly his conveyance was on what we might term "the American plan", being foddered night and morning at no extra charge.

The price of meals varied likewise. The same Bill of Fare lists:

A hot diet, well dressed . . . 1 shilling.

A hot diet, presumably, was something of an 18th-century "blue plate special" consisting of some substantial meat stew, bread, and a two-quart mug of "small" beer. For gentlemen who may feel somewhat put down that their ancestors could consume such quantities of this beverage, "small" beer is here defined: 'twas a poor substitute for the real thing, fermented for a brief period and, therefore, low in alcoholic content as contrasted with strong beer. Thus, it was generally the beverage of the poor who could afford nothing better. Logically.

Q. What is an Ordinary?

A. An old term synonymous with tavern and inn; although ordinaries were more often for dining purposes, usually having limited accommodations for overnight. Felicity recalls a sour note read in some fastidious foreign traveler's journal. He wrote, "The ordinaries here, and they are all just that, leave much for the weary traveler to desire".

****

TAXES
****

We are compelled to mention this odious word for so many visitors inquire.

Q. Does Colonial Williamsburg pay taxes?

A. Being a non-profit, philanthropic, educational foundation with a staggering loss of over a million dollars a year, income taxes are eliminated so far as the educational properties are concerned. Real estate taxes are paid locally on all properties owned by the Foundation (with the exception of major exhibition buildings, the Information Center and the Folk Art Museum—all educational). In recent years, official figures indicate real estate taxes to the city of Williamsburg paid by the Foundation exceed one third of the total tax revenue. Now, let us hasten to another subject which, unfortunately is also an unpopular one in our day.

****

TERMITES

****

Q. Didn't they have them back then?

A. Oh, yes. Termites are not a modern invention. We inquired regarding this interesting question, having noted ourselves the soundness of joists, beams, studs and clapboards of old houses. We were told that houses were less attractive to termites in those days because of prodigious piles of firewood stacked some distances from them and the vast amount of natural rotting wood in a land of far-reaching virgin timber. This seems logical, does it not?

****

TOOLS

****

Q. What kind of tools did they have to produce all of this fine paneling, carving and moulding?

A. Oh, far better than an answer, dear reader, is to avail oneself of the privilege of observing the local cabinetmaker. You will note that tools have changed but little since colonial days. The matter of power production with which they were operated is the most striking difference. Where we use the energy of electricity, steam, gas and atoms, our ancestors were obliged to use their own.

- 88 -

****

TREES

****

This subject, like furnishings, ceramics, metals and the like is so vast and Felicity's knowledge so limited, she cannot treat it adequately here. There are excellent books available, of course, for visitors having more than a passing interest. Included here are five brief "tree answers" for those who have but a passing interest.

Paper Mulberry Tree

Q. What are those funny looking old gnarled trees?

A. Paper Mulberry. It is characteristic of this tree, as it ages, to grow so.

This triggers an unpleasant thought to all of us past forty, does it not? However, if the visitor has seen everything in Williamsburg but has more time to spend, Felicity suggests a fascinating diversion. Stroll through the city looking at these curious trees much as one watches clouds, allowing the imagination to suggest all manner of people and objects. You will find this a unique amusement if you have a good imagination. Undoubtedly.

Q. What are the trees which seem to have no bark but produce those beautiful pink (also white and lavender) clusters ail summer?

A. Crape myrtle, and is indeed beautiful in full summer bloom; but it is almost as interesting sans leaves and blossoms in winter because of the very smooth greyish bark and growth pattern. Felicity is pained to disappoint visitors living above Baltimore since Crape myrtle is a "suthenah". However, some very successful gardeners can grow them, in very sheltered locations, as far north as New York City. They are cultivated in the southwest with tender loving care.

Q. What are the tall trees with huge waxy leaves and gorgeous white blossoms?

A. These, deah readah, are just common ol' suthen mag-nol-ya. Felicity teases. Magnolia Grandiflora is native, evergreen and produces the huge white blossoms in summer. It sometimes reaches the majestic height of 80 feet or more. Please do not yearn for one if you live above Washington, D.C.—or Philadelphia, where we are told extreme kindness occasionally induces a few to survive, if not thrive.

Q. What are the trees in front of the Palace with those big green fruits?

A. Osage orange; but please do not let the name mislead you. The fruit will stay green and is not edible. The Indians of the southwest, where the tree is indigenous, prized its very strong wood and used it for clubs and bows. It was also a source for orange and green dyes.

Q. What are the trees bordering Palace Green with those long beans hanging from the branches?

A. Catalpas. Colonial Virginians borrowed them too. Some catalpas are native to the Gulf States and the so-called "western" catalpa, over to Arkansas and up to Illinois. It is believed Indians smoked the long pods for they were known as "cigar trees" and "smoking bean trees". Felicity does not recommend this. The result, she is told, is unpleasant (if permitted to coin another word)—something like "catal-pot". Please excuse me.

****

UNDERWEAR
(See COSTUMES)

****

VOLUNTEERS

****

Q. Are you ladies volunteers or members of some organization?

A. The question came up earlier under the heading, LADIES, and we promised to make a more detailed and less emphatic answer which is still "no".

As explained in the topic of TRAINING, whether a Host's or Hostess's schedule is full or part time, the work definitely is not as easy as it appears to the visitor who sees the beautiful costumes and surroundings. The costumed interpreter is attempting to make your experience here both pleasant and enlightening, all at the same time. Sheer numbers often render this a most fatiguing task. For, in addition to his own fatigue, the interpreter is concerned about the visitors' fatigue, time schedules and interests. Groups are composed of a number of people with different time schedules and interests. Knowing this, the interpreter is keenly conscious, if the author may paraphrase an old saying, that they can please some of the people all the time, all the people some of the time; but never all the people all the time.

Kind readers, please believe then, that a Hostess, Host or other interpreter's greatest satisfaction is in ratio to how much he or she is able to please YOU, either by entertainment, enlightenment or both. Hopefully.

Note: An exquisite example: A little boy in a predominately adult group having endured a lengthy tour of the Capitol, remarked, "Gee, I liked this 'cause I've been interested in history all my life."

"How old are you?", asked the Hostess.

"I'm seven and in the second grade." he proudly replied.

****

WATER

****

Q. Where can we get a drink of?

Water Fountain

A. It is not scarce. It is just not where you would usually look for it as in the case with REST ROOMS. Felicity suggests a pleasant little game unless, of course, one is too thirsty to play. In this case, it is advisable to inquire of the location of the nearest drinking fountain. Otherwise, look in barrels and well houses about the area. 'Tis like an Easter Egg hunt but for finding water fountains rather than eggs.

****

WAX
(See FLOORS)

****

WHITE WALLS
(See PAINTS

****

WIGS
(See COSTUMES)

****

****
WHY
****

Q. Why was WILLIAMSBURG restored?

A. First, it played such an important part in the days when America was having its birth pangs. As before mentioned, other such important political centers of the same historic period are now metropolitan areas, making such a project impossible. The real concept of the dream of the late Dr. W. A. R. Goodwin who interested Mr. Rockefeller in the project is to preserve our heritage by ever reminding Americans of the integrity of the individual, responsible leadership, self-government, individual liberty and opportunity. Mr. Rockefeller thought, as did Patrick Henry and earlier philosophers, that the future can learn from the past. We are the future of that past as we will be the past of our own childrens' future. There are lessons to be learned from history, the good and the bad of it.

Felicity does not sermonize. She adds, however, one quote to ponder. It is Point XV of THE VIRGINIA DECLARATION OF RIGHTS written by George Mason and adopted in Virginia June 12, 1776.

"No free Government, or the Blessings of Liberty can be preserved to any People, but by a firm Adherence to Justice, Moderation, Temperance, Frugality, and Virtue and by frequent Recurrence to fundamental Principles."

****
X, Y, and Z
****

After several excruciating hours of intellectual labor, we concluded visitors seldom ask X, Y, and Z questions. However, because there occurs an exquisite sensation of pain upon being thus forced to end this trifling work, we leave the reader (unless, alas, the reader has long since left us) with the following sentiment.

Felicity fervently hopes we are no longer (to borrow a word from the ancient Greeks) ZENOS (strangers) because YOU, dear reader, became her friend when you purchased this little volume; and, hopefully, it may have flavored your visit to the past here with a tiny touch of ZEST.

So fondly, adieu
Felicity